ADVANCED GUIDE TO RECRUITMENT

DR. MOHAMMED BAWAJI

ISBN 979-888591377-5

By my soul and my heart, I dedicate my efforts to the

epitomes of knowledge:

The 52nd Dai Al Mutlaq,

His Holiness Dr. Syedna Mohammed Burhanuddin R.A. &

his Successor

The 53rd Dai Al Mutlaq, Leader of the Dawoodi Bohra

community worldwide.

His Holiness Dr. Syedna Mufaddal Saifuddin T.U.S.

Contents

ADVANCED GUIDE TO RECRUITMENT

"Acquiring the right talent and nurturing them is the art of an expert recruiter"

About The Author

Dr Mohammed Bawaji, HR Strategist, Speaker, Author and Entrepreneur

For over a decade Dr. Mohammed Bawaji has been not only an entrepreneur but a pioneer in developing transformational HR processes and written seven books for corporate and academic use. While he is constantly intrigued by HR and its processes, he has also developed numerous short online courses and is also a consultant on topic related to career and education. A strategic human resource specialist, career coach and educationalist, Dr Bawaji serves as a recruitment advisor to many Fortune 500 companies. The Economic Times has nominated him for the coveted title 'Leader for Tomorrow" for three consecutive years (2010-2012). He is the only trainer to be to be certified by TUV SUD South Asia Pacific Pvt Ltd. (A German-based auditing firm) for the Programme in Entrepreneurship Development. (PED) in 2016.

Becoming an author was not something Dr Bawaji had always planned. Having grown up battling SLD, a disorder that limited his learning and reading abilities, he found ways to cope and live with his condition while making the most out of his situation. At a point in his life he realised his aptitude for writing was significant and he was not only passionate but driven to write on topics of interest. That's when his first book **'Human Resource Principles and Functions"** got published in 2010 and went on to become a bestseller for academic use. This put him on the list of the handful of Maharashtrian writers for a South Indian University. His next book **"Strategic Human Resource Management"** aimed at PG students earned him a nomination for the '**Youngest Author**" to have written on the topic in 2018 by Nirali and Pragati Publications. In 2015, his company CPHR Services Pvt Ltd was awarded 2nd place among the top 20 most promising HROs by Silicon Magazine.

His latest book **"Transformational HR-Beyond Processes"** is based on a phenomenal HR concept and a single diagram called "**HR Process Effectiveness Tool**" that he curated. This book is available for purchase on the company's website and other online portals. It includes twenty-one elements of HR processes and each of these has an explanatory corresponding diagram. Furthermore, these chapters are summarised in a snapshot format for an easy read. Perhaps the most unique thing he has added to the mix is supplementing these snapshots with a video tutorial.

An innovative way to approach reading, Mr Bawaji has not left any stone unturned in making sure his readers get the most in

Currently he is working on his new book that shows how the twenty-one elements of the HR Process Effectiveness Tool can be quantified the help of maturity matrices. This is a further elaboration of HR processes which includes nearly 127 measurable elements.

When he isn't busy coming up with new ways to develop HR processes, Dr Bawaji provides consultation to individuals on education and career planning and decision making. With many success stories he is a well sought out counsellor in his community and outside as well.

Dr. Bawaji is interested in exploring potential symbiotic relationships to address the growing need for implementation of HR Processes on a corporate and academic level globally.

Overview- Advanced Recruitment

Advanced recruitment Book helps to understand the importance of recruitment and the various steps to be taken to ensure an appropriate supply of human resources in an organisation.

Recruitment is the most productive asset to an organisation. The important objective of recruitment is to attract people in multi-dimensional skills & experiences. Once the candidate is recruited and becomes a part of the organization, the manager must conduct performance appraisal based on his work performance.

Performance Appraisal offers a valuable opportunity to focus on work activities and goals, to identify and correct existing problems, and to encourage better future performance. Thus the performance of the whole organisation is enhanced.

Managers must give due importance to forecasting. It helps in assessing an organisation's current human resource situation to project future demand for the same. Forecasting helps in manpower planning.

Manpower planning is the process of deciding the various openings available in the company and how they need to be filled. It takes care of company's present and future vacancies – right from the front office staff to the clerks till the President and the CEO.

One of the vital tasks to be considered in the process of recruitment is budgeting as it helps to use the available funds in an appropriate manner. Budgeting helps to make educated guesses as to how much money will be needed to get the next fiscal year's recruitment efforts off the ground.

Every organisation must carry out competency mapping for its smooth functioning. Competency mapping is the process of identifying the competencies (technical, managerial, behavioural,

conceptual knowledge, attitudes, skills, etc.) required to successfully perform a given job or role

at a given point of time.

CHAPTER ONE

Recruitment

It is a process to discover the sources of manpower to meet the requirements of the organisation. Recruitment is the most productive asset/ resource to an organisation. The important objective of requirement is to attract people in multi-dimensional skills & experiences that suit the present and future organizational needs. The basic purpose of recruiting is to develop a group of potentially qualified people.

Suitability for a job is typically assessed by looking for skills, e.g. communication skills, technical abilities, computer skills, leadership skills. Evidence for skills required for a job may be provided in the form of qualifications (educational or professional), experience in a job requiring the relevant skills or the testimony of references. Employment agencies may also give computerized tests to assess an individual's "off-hand" knowledge of software packages or typing skills. At a more basic level written tests may be given to assess numeracy and literacy. A candidate may also be assessed on the basis of an interview. Sometimes candidates will be requested to provide a resume or to complete a Job application form to provide this evidence.

The follow-up process may be referred to as part of the recruitment process: convincing the selected candidate or candidates to take up the target job or function.

RECRUITMENT PROCESS

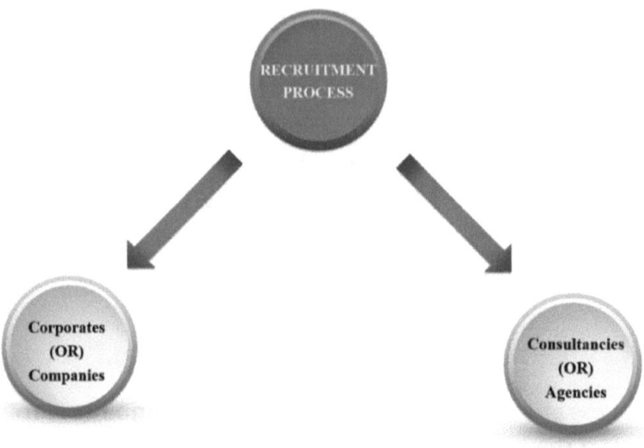

- **Recruitment in Corporates/Companies**

Recruitment in corporates is different from that of consultancies. In case of any requirement: Give advertisement on job portals, various Medias, Campus recruitments and also through their own websites etc.

1. After receiving the application, Screening and scrutinize appropriate resumes.
2. Calling them for interviews.
3. Conducting various levels of interviews like attitude, aptitude, Stress interviews and physical examination etc.
4. If the candidate seems to be suitable then selecting them.

FLOWCHART FOR RECRUITMENT IN COMPANIES

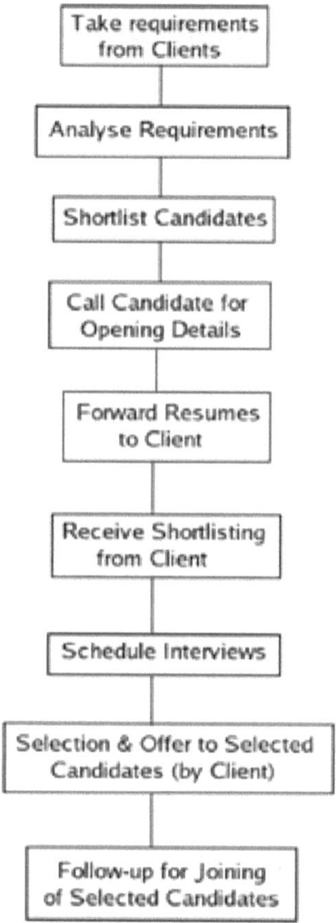

- **Recruitment in Consultancies**

Private employment agencies or consultants perform the recruitment functions on behalf of a client company by charging fee. Line managers are relieved from recruitment functions so that they can concentrate on their operational activities and recruitment functions is entrusted to the consultants. Consultancies function effectively in the recruitment of executives. Hence, they are also called executive search agencies. Most of the organizations depend on this source for highly specialized positions and executive positions.

FLOWCHART FOR RECRUITMENT IN CONSULTANCIES

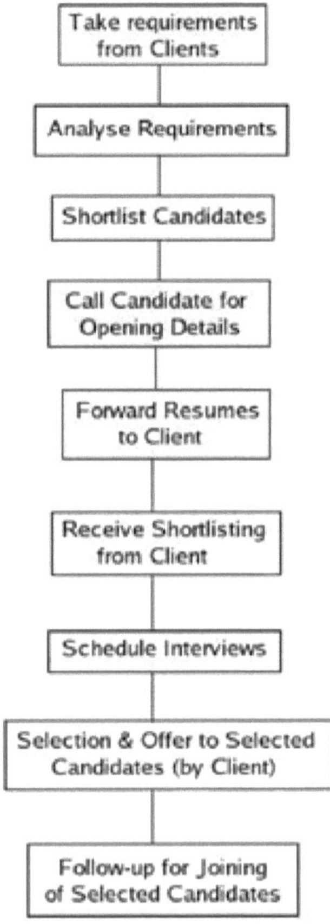

TESTING FOR EMPLOYMENT

Testing for Employment includes:

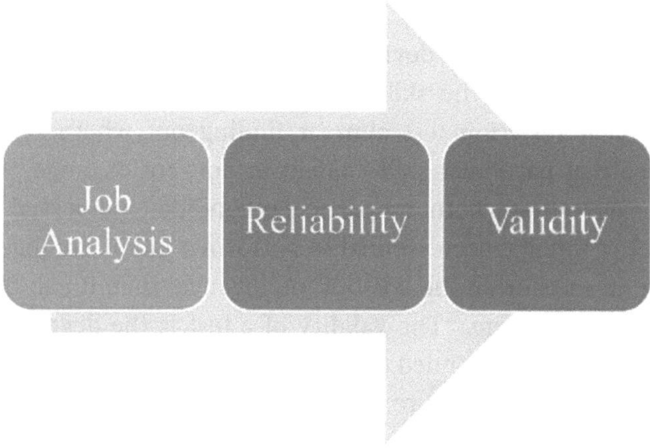

1. **Job Analysis:** One of the important testing concepts is job analysis as it provides basic information about the type of the candidates needed by the organization. Job specification and job requirements provide information about the demands made by a job on the incumbent, whereas employee specification gives the information about the characteristics, qualities, behavior of the employees needed to perform a job successfully. Thus, employee specification is the basis to decide upon a particular test or tests and minimum acceptable score in order to test whether the candidates possessed the required amount and degree of behavior and qualities like intelligence, aptitude to perform the job successfully.
2. **Reliability:** After identifying the test(s), the administrator of test should ensure the reliability of test / instrument. Reliability of a test refers to the level of consistency of score or results obtained throughout a series of measurements. If a person obtains same or similar score in the tests conducted in first, second and third time, under the same conditions, it is said the test is reliable. The reliability of any selection technique / test refers to its freedom from systematic errors of measurements or its consistency under different conditions. A test is unreliable if the score differs considerably in first, second and third measurements. The causes of low reliability are: conducting the rest under non-standardized conditions, administering the test by different persons and under

different psychological states of candidate, existence of factor of luck and ill- luck etc.

3. **Validity:** Any selection device should aim at finding out whether a candidate possessed the skills or talents required by a particular job or not. Each selection test aims at finding out whether a candidate possessed that particular skill / talent or not. For example, intelligence test aims at testing whether a particular candidate possessed the nature and level of intelligence essential to perform a job. If intelligence test is effective in measuring the level of intelligence, then it can be said that the test is a valid one. "The validity of a test is the degree to which it measures what it is intended to measure. A valid test predicts accurately the level of success or failure of a candidate on the job.

After the tests' reliability and validity are tested, the personnel manager has to develop testing programs. The following steps can be followed in installing testing programs:

1. Formulation of the objectives of testing programs.
2. Analysis of jobs to identify those characteristics that appears necessary for job success.
3. Making of a tentative choice of tests for a try-out.
4. Administering of those tests to an experimental group of people.
5. Establishing of criteria for job success.
6. Analysis of results and making of decisions regarding test application.

TESTING TERMINOLOGY

- A minimum score is that which generally shall at least twice as large as a chance score.
- A chance score is one which can be obtained even if a person knows nothing about test's subject –matter.
- A norm is the percentage of people who get less than or equal to certain scores.
- Alternatives form means two or more versions of the same test which are identical in length, difficulty and type of coverage of questions but whose specific questions are different.

- A multiple choice test s one in which two or more possible choices are limited
- A true or false test contains a list of statements and the candidate given the test indicates which are true and which are false.
- A completion test contains sentences of one or more words or facts omitted, the task of the candidate giving the test is to insert the missing word or fact.
- An equivalency test is one of knowledge which indicates whether an applicant without the prescribed education or experience has the knowledge implied by an educational or work standard.
- An omnibus test is one which, although it contains diverse items, provides only a single score.
- A test battery means that the applicant is required to take two or more tests, each, individually-timed, scored and weighted.
- A work limit test is one in which the applicant is permitted to finish the given work and the amount of time he takes is recorded.
- A time-limit test is one in which the applicant is permitted to take fixed time and the amount of work he finishes is recorded.

TYPES OF SELECTION TESTS

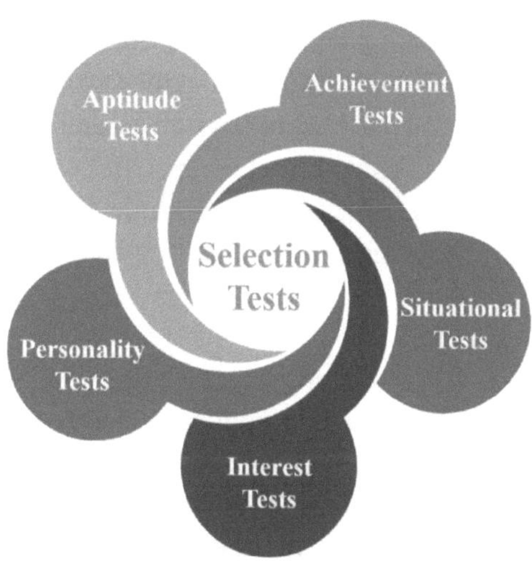

I. **Aptitude Tests:**

These tests measure whether an individual has the capacity or latent ability to learn a given job if given adequate training. Aptitudes can be divided into general and mental ability or intelligence and specific aptitude such as mechanical, clerical, manipulative capacity etc.

a. **Intelligence Tests:** These tests in general measure intelligence quotient of a candidates. In detail these tests measure capacity for comprehension, reasoning, word fluency,

verbal comprehension, numbers, memory and space .Other factors such as digit spans— both forward and backward, information known, comprehension, vocabulary, picture arrangement and object assembly.

Though these tests are accepted as useful ones, they are criticized against deprived sections of the community. Further, it is also criticized that these tests may prove to be too dull as a selection device.

a. **Mechanical Aptitude Tests:** These tests measure the capacities of spatial visualization, perceptual speed and knowledge of mechanical matter. These tests are useful for selecting apprentices, skilled, mechanical employees, technicians etc.
b. **Psychomotor Tests:** These tests measure abilities like manual dexterity, motor ability and eye-hand coordination of candidates. These tests are useful to select semi-skilled workers and workers for repetitive operations like packing, watch assembly.
c. **Clerical Aptitude Tests:** Measure specific capacities involved in office work. Items of this test include spelling, computation, comprehension, copying, word measuring etc.

II. Achievement Tests:

These tests are conducted when applicant claims to know something as these tests are concerned with what one has accomplished These tests are more useful to measure the value of specific achievement when an organization wishes to employ experienced candidates. These tests are classified into:

a. **Job Knowledge Test:** Under this test a candidate is tested in the knowledge of a particular job. For example, if a junior lecturer applies for the job of a senior lecturer in commerce, he may be tested in job knowledge where he is asked questions about Accountancy principle, Banking, Law, Business Management etc.
b. **Work Sample Test:** Under this test a portion of the actual work is given to the candidates as a test and the candidate is asked to do it. If a candidate applies for a post of lecturer in Management he may be asked to deliver a lecture on Management Information System as work sample test.

Thus, the candidate's achievement in his career is tested regarding his knowledge about the job and actual work experience.

III. Situational Test:

This test evaluates a candidate in a similar real life situation. In this test the candidates is asked either to cope with the situation or solve critical situations of the job. These are:

a. **Group Discussion:** This test is administered through group discussion approach to solve a problem under which candidates are observed in the areas of initiating, leading, proposing valuable ideas, conciliating skills, oral communicating skills, coordinating and concluding skills.
b. **In Basket:** The candidate, in this test, is supplied with actual letters, telephone and telegraphic message, reports and requirements by various officers of the organization, adequate information about the job and organization. The candidates is asked to take decisions on various items based on the in basket information regarding requirements in the memoranda.

IV. Interest Tests:

These tests are inventories of the likes and dislikes of candidates in relation to work, job, occupations, hobbies and recreational activities. The purposes of this test is to find out whether a candidate is interested or disinterested in the job for which he is a candidate and to find out in which area of the job range/occupation the candidate is interested. The assumption of this test is

that there is a high correlation between the interest of a candidate in a job and job success. Interest inventories are less faked and they may not fluctuate after the age of 30.

V. Personality Tests:

These tests prove deeply to discover clues to an individual's value system, his emotional reactions and maturity and characteristic mood. They are expressed in such traits like self- confidence, tact, emotional control, optimism, decisiveness, sociability, conformity, objectivity, patience, fear, distrust, initiative, judgment dominance or submission, impulsiveness, sympathy, integrity, stability and self-confidence.

a. **Objective Tests:** Most personality tests are objective tests as they are suitable for group testing and can be scored objectively.

b. **Projective Tests:** Candidates are asked to project their own interpretation of certain standard stimulus situations basing on ambiguous pictures, figures etc., under these tests.

Personality tests have disadvantage in the sense that they can be faked by sophisticated candidates and most candidates give socially acceptable answers. Further, personality inventories may not successfully predict job success.

Further, we can also classify tests according to whether they measure cognitive (mental) abilities, motor and physical abilities, personality and interests or achievements.

Cognitive tests include tests of general reasoning ability (intelligence) and tests of specific mental abilities like memory and inductive reasoning.

IQ Tests:

Intelligence (IQ) tests are tests of general intellectual abilities. They measure not a single trait but rather a range of abilities, including memory, vocabulary, verbal fluency and numerical ability.

Originally, IQ (intelligence quotient) was literally a quotient. The procedure was to divide a child's mental age (as measured by the intelligence test) by his or her chronological age, and then multiply the results by 100. If an 8 year old child answered questions as a 10-year-old might, his or her IQ would be 10 divided by 8 times 100 or 125.

For adults, of course, the notion of mental age divided by chronological age wouldn't make sense. Therefore, an adult's IQ score is actually a derived score. It reflects the extent to which the person is above or below the 'average' adult's intelligence score.

Intelligence is often measured with individually administered tests like the Stanford-Binet test or the Wechsler Test. Employers can administer other IQ tests such as the Wobderlic to groups of people. Other intelligence tests include the Kaufman Adolescent and Adult Intelligence Test, the Slosson Intelligence Test, the Wide Range Intelligence Test and the Comprehensive Test of Nonverbal Intelligence.

Specific Cognitive Abilities:

There are also measures of specific mental abilities, such as inductive and deductive reasoning, verbal comprehension, memory, and numerical ability.

Psychologists often call such tests aptitude tests, since they purport to measure aptitude for the job in question. Consider the Test of Mechanical Comprehension in which tests the applicants' understanding of basic mechanical principles. It may reflect a person's aptitude for jobs like that of machinist or engineer that require mechanical comprehension. Other tests of mechanical aptitude include the Mechanical Reasoning Test and the SRA Test of Mechanical Aptitude. The revised Minnesota Paper Form Board Test consists of 64 two-dimensional diagrams cut into separate pieces. It provides insights into an applicant's mechanical spatial ability; you'd use it

for screening applicants for jobs such as designers, drafts-people, or engineers.

Tests of Motor and Physical Abilities:

There may be a need to measure motor abilities, such as finger dexterity, manual dexterity, and reaction time. The Crawford Small Parts Dexterity Test is an example. It measures the speed and accuracy of simple judgment as well as the speed of finger, hand, and arm movements. Other tests here include the Stromberg Dexterity Test, the Minnesota Rate of Manipulation Test, and the Purdue Peg Board. The Roeder Manipulative Aptitude Test screens individuals for jobs where dexterity is a main requirement. Finger dexterity tests are conducted for small assembly products like telecom instruments, switchgear, PCs, watches where even both hands right as well as left come into action simultaneously.

Tests of physical abilities may also be required. These include static strength (such as lifting weights), dynamic strength (like pull-ups), body coordination (as in jumping rope), and stamina. Lifeguards, for example must show they can swim a course before they're hired.

Selection of personnel for an organization is a crucial, complex and continuing function. The ability of an organization to attain its goals effectively and to develop in a dynamic environment largely depends upon the effectiveness of its selection programs. In a situation where the right person is not selected, the remaining functions of personnel management, employee-employer relations will not be effective. If the right person is selected, he/she is a valuable asset to the organization and if faulty selection is made, the employee will become a liability to the organization.

INTERVIEW PROCESS

Interview is not a single step. It is a process consisting of several steps. The major steps are grouped into four categories:

I. **Preparation for the Interview:** Advance preparation for interview is essential as it permits focusing its coverage on the vital aspects and its helps the interviewer to remember and absorb many impressions and facts. The following preparation has to be made by the organization before starting an interview.

i. Choose the appropriate types of interviews based on job requirements and the nature of the interviews discussed earlier.
ii. Identify the knowledge, skill area to be examined through interviews based on job requirements.
iii. Determine the type and number of interviewers: Interviewers should be selected based on personal characteristics, technical competence, initiative common sense, general smartness, ability to inspire confidence, capacity to work in a team and potential for growth.

Interviewers may be drawn from personnel specialists, line managers concerned experts in the discipline concerned, from academicians, practitioners and psychologists.

i. Review of the information collected in advance through other selection methods, finding out the validity of those methods, the score obtained etc. The information available in the application blank should be thoroughly checked regarding:

- Accuracy and validity.
- Acquainting about the applicant.
- To find out stability, review the no: of positions and length of time held in each of the past jobs.
- Compare the nature of positions in the previous employment with that of proposed employment.
- Check the employee growth with the organizational progression in the past employment
- Find out discharges etc. through unexplained breaks.

This helps in avoiding further evaluation of those areas appraised effectively by other means through interviews.

v. Decide upon the administrative arrangements.

vi. Finalize the physical setting including time which would be convenient to interviewees and interviewers.
vii. Determine the coverage of the interview: Generally the interview should cover the areas like relevance of qualification and experience to job requirements, gaps in employment history and causes therefore, reasons for choosing course, school, occupation etc. likes and dislikes sense of humor, quickness of reaction, ability to recognize thoughts, manner and poise, cultural level etc.
viii. Find out the conditions under which the interview technique is effective This includes:

- Consistency in the results of various selection techniques.
- Use the interview technique to test the candidate in those areas where other techniques are ineffective.
- When the purpose of the interview is to find out the most suitable position to the applicant.

TYPES OF INTERVIEWS

All job interviews have the same objective, but employers reach that objective in a variety of ways. You might enter the room expecting to tell stories about your professional successes and instead find yourself selling the interviewer a bridge or editing code at a computer. One strategy for performing your best during an interview is to know the rules of the particular game you are playing when you walk through the door.

1. The Screening Interview

Companies use screening tools to ensure that candidates meet minimum qualification requirements. Computer programs are among the tools used to weed out unqualified candidates. Sometimes human professionals are the gatekeepers. Screening interviewers often have honed skills to determine whether there is anything that might disqualify you for the position.

Remember - they do not need to know whether you are the best fit for the position, only whether you are not a match. For this reason, screeners tend to dig for dirt. Screeners will hone in on gaps in your employment history or pieces of information that look inconsistent. They also will want to know from the outset whether you will be too expensive for the company.

Some tips for maintaining confidence during screening interviews:

- Highlight your accomplishments and qualifications.
- Get into the straightforward groove. Personality is not as important to the screener as verifying your qualifications. Answer questions directly and succinctly. Save your winning personality for the person making hiring decisions!
- Be tactful about addressing income requirements. Give a range, and try to avoid giving specifics by replying, "I would be willing to consider your best offer."
- If the interview is conducted by phone, it is helpful to have note cards with your vital information sitting next to the phone. That way, whether the interviewer catches you sleeping or vacuuming the floor, you will be able to switch gears quickly.

2. The Informational Interview:

On the opposite end of the stress spectrum from screening interviews is the informational interview. A meeting that you initiate, the informational interview is underutilized by job- seekers who might otherwise consider themselves savvy to the merits of networking. Job seekers ostensibly secure informational meetings in order to seek the advice of someone in their current or desired field as well as to gain further references to people who can lend insight.

Employers that like to stay apprised of available talent even when they do not have current job openings, are often open to informational interviews, especially if they like to share their knowledge, feel flattered by your interest, or esteem the mutual friend that connected you to them. During an informational interview, the jobseeker and employer exchange information and get to know one another better without reference to a specific job opening.

This takes off some of the performance pressure, but be intentional nonetheless:

- Come prepared with thoughtful questions about the field and the company.

- Gain references to other people and make sure that the interviewer would be comfortable if you contact other people and use his or her name.
- Give the interviewer your card, contact information and resume.
- Write a thank you note to the interviewer.

3. The Directive Style Interview:

In this style of interview, the interviewer has a clear agenda that he or she follows unflinchingly. Sometimes companies use this rigid format to ensure parity between interviews; when interviewers ask each candidate the same series of questions, they can more readily compare the results. Directive interviewers rely upon their own questions and methods to tease from you what they wish to know. You might feel like you are being steam-rolled, or you might find the conversation develops naturally. Their style does not necessarily mean that they have dominance issues, although you should keep an eye open for these if the interviewer would be your supervisor.

Either way, remember:

- Flex with the interviewer, following his or her lead.
- Do not relinquish complete control of the interview. If the interviewer does not ask you for information that you think is important to proving your superiority as a candidate, politely interject it.

4. The Meandering Style Interview:

This interview type, usually used by inexperienced interviewers, relies on you to lead the discussion. It might begin with a statement like "tell me about yourself," which you can use to your advantage. The interviewer might ask you another broad, open-ended question before falling into silence. This interview style allows you tactfully to guide the discussion in a way that best serves you.

The following strategies, which are helpful for any interview, are particularly important when interviewers use a non-directive approach:

- Come to the interview prepared with highlights and anecdotes of your skills, qualities and experiences. Do not rely on the interviewer to spark your memory-jot down some notes that you can reference throughout the interview.

- Remain alert to the interviewer. Even if you feel like you can take the driver's seat and go in any direction you wish, remain respectful of the interviewer's role. If he or she becomes more directive during the interview, adjust.
- Ask well-placed questions. Although the open format allows you significantly to shape the interview, running with your own agenda and dominating the conversation means that you run the risk of missing important information about the company and its needs.

5. The Stress Interview:

Astounding as this is, the Greek hazing system has made its way into professional interviews. Either employers view the stress interview as a legitimate way of determining candidates' aptness for a position or someone has latent maniacal tendencies. You might be held in the waiting room for an hour before the interviewer greets you. You might face long silences or cold stares. The interviewer might openly challenge your believes or judgment. You might be called upon to perform an impossible task on the fly-like convincing the interviewer to exchange shoes with you. Insults and miscommunication are common. All this is designed to see whether you have the mettle to withstand the company culture, the clients or other potential stress.

Besides wearing a strong anti-perspirant, you will do well to:

- Remember that this is a game. It is not personal. View it as the surreal interaction that it is.
- Prepare and memorize your main message before walking through the door. If you are flustered, you will better maintain clarity of mind if you do not have to wing your responses.
- Even if the interviewer is rude, remain calm and tactful.

Go into the interview relaxed and rested. If you go into it feeling stressed, you will have a more difficult time keeping a cool perspective.

6. The Behavioral Interview:

Many companies increasingly rely on behavior interviews since they use your previous behavior to indicate your future performance. In these interviews, employers use standardized methods to mine information relevant to your competency in a particular area or position.

Depending upon the responsibilities of the job and the working environment, you might be asked to describe a time that required problem-solving skills, adaptability, leadership, conflict resolution, multi-tasking, initiative or stress management. You will be asked how you dealt with the situations.

Your responses require not only reflection, but also organization. To maximize your responses in the behavioral format:

- Anticipate the transferable skills and personal qualities that are required for the job.
- Review your resume. Any of the qualities and skills you have included in your resume are fair game for an interviewer to press.
- Reflect on your own professional, volunteer, educational and personal experience to develop brief stories that highlight these skills and qualities in you. You should have a story for each of the competencies on your resume as well as those you anticipate the job requires.
- Prepare stories by identifying the context, logically highlighting your actions in the situation. Keep your responses concise & present them in less than two minutes.

7. The Audition:

For some positions, such as computer programmers or trainers, companies want to see you in action before they make their decision. For this reason, they might take you through a simulation or brief exercise in order to evaluate your skills. An audition can be enormously useful to you as well, since it allows you to demonstrate your abilities in interactive ways that are likely familiar to you. The simulations and exercises should also give you a simplified sense of what the job would be like. If you sense that other candidates have an edge on you in terms of experience or other qualifications, requesting an audition can help level the playing field.

To maximize on auditions, remember to:

1. Clearly understand the instructions and expectations for the exercise. Communication is half the battle in real life, and you should demonstrate to the prospective employer that you make the effort to do things right the first time by minimizing confusion.
2. Treat the situation as if you are a professional with responsibility for the task laid before you. Take ownership of your work.
3. Brush up on your skills before an interview if you think they might be tested.

8. The Group Interview:

Interviewing simultaneously with other candidates can be disconcerting, but it provides the company with a sense of your leadership potential and style. The group interview helps the company get a glimpse of how you interact with peers-are you timid or bossy, are you attentive or do you seek attention, do others turn to you instinctively, or do you compete for authority? The interviewer also wants to view what your tools of persuasion are: do you use argumentation and careful reasoning to gain support or do you divide and conquer? The interviewer might call on you to discuss an issue with the other candidates, solve a problem collectively, or discuss your peculiar qualifications in front of the other candidates.

This environment might seem overwhelming or hard to control, but there are a few tips that will help you navigate the group interview successfully:

- Observe to determine the dynamics the interviewer establishes and try to discern the rules of the game. If you are unsure of what is expected from you, ask for clarification from the interviewer.
- Treat others with respect while exerting influence over others.
- Avoid overt power conflicts, which will make you look uncooperative and immature.
- Keep an eye on the interviewer throughout the process so that you do not miss important cues.

9. The Tag-Team Interview:

Expecting to meet with Ms. Glenn, you might find yourself in a room with four other people: Ms. Glenn, two of her staff, and the Sales Director.

Companies often want to gain the insights of various people when interviewing candidates. This method of interviewing is often attractive for companies that rely heavily on team cooperation. Not only does the company want to know whether your skills balance that of the company, but also whether you can get along with the other workers. In some companies, multiple people will interview you simultaneously. In other companies, you will proceed through a series of one-on-one interviews.

Some helpful tips for maximizing on this interview format:

- Treat each person as an important individual. Gain each person's business card at the beginning of the meeting, if possible, and refer to each person by name. If there are several people in the room at once, you might wish to scribble down their names on a sheet of paper according to where each is sitting. Make eye contact with each person and speak directly to the person asking each question.

- Use the opportunity to gain as much information about the company as you can. Just as each interviewer has a different function in the company, they each have a unique perspective. When asking questions, be sensitive not to place anyone in a position that invites him to compromise confidentiality or loyalty.
- Bring at least double the anecdotes and sound-bites to the interview as you would for a traditional one-on-one interview. Be ready to illustrate your main message in a variety of ways to a variety of people.
- Prepare psychologically to expend more energy and be more alert than you would in a one-on- one interview. Stay focused and adjustable.

10. The Mealtime Interview:

For many, interviewing over a meal sounds like a professional and digestive catastrophe in the making. If you have difficulty chewing gum while walking, this could be a challenge. With some preparation and psychological readjustment, you can enjoy the process. Meals often have a cementing social effect-breaking bread together tends to facilitate deals, marriages, friendships, and religious communion. Mealtime interviews rely on this logic, and expand it.

Particularly when your job requires interpersonal acuity, companies want to know what you are like in a social setting. Are you relaxed and charming or awkward and evasive? Companies want to observe not only how you handle a fork, but also how you treat your host, any other guests, and the serving staff.

Some basic social tips help ease the complexity of mixing food with business:

- Take cues from your interviewer, remembering that you are the guest. Do not sit down until your host does. Order something slightly less extravagant than your interviewer. If he badly wants you to try a particular dish, oblige him. If he recommends an appetizer to you, he likely intends to order one himself. Do not begin eating until he does. If he orders coffee and dessert, do not leave him eating alone.
- If your interviewer wants to talk business, do so. If she and the other guests discuss their upcoming travel plans or their families, do not launch into business.
- Try to set aside dietary restrictions and preferences. Remember, the interviewer is your host. It is rude to be finicky unless you absolutely must. If you must, be as tactful as you can. Avoid phrases like: "I do not eat mammals," or "Shrimp makes my eyes swell and water."
- Choose manageable food items, if possible. Avoid barbeque ribs and spaghetti.
- Find a discrete way to check your teeth after eating. Excuse yourself from the table for a moment.
- Practice eating and discussing something important simultaneously.
- Thank your interviewer for the meal.

11. The Follow-up Interview:

Companies bring candidates back for second and sometimes third or fourth interviews for a number of reasons. Sometimes they just want to confirm that you are the amazing worker they first thought you to be. Sometimes they are having difficulty deciding between a short-list of candidates. Other times, the interviewer's supervisor or other decision makers in the company want to gain a sense of you before signing a hiring decision.

The second interview could go in a variety of directions, and you must prepare for each of them. When meeting with the same person again, you do not need to be as assertive in your communication of your skills. You can focus on cementing rapport, understanding where the company is going and how your skills mesh with the company vision and culture. Still, the interviewer should view you as the answer to their needs. You might find yourself negotiating a compensation package. Alternatively, you might find that you are starting with a new person.

Administering the Interview Process

Interviews can also be administered in various ways: one on one or by a panel of interviewers; sequentially or all at once; and computerized or personally

Personal or individual Interviews:

Most interviews are individual or one-on-one: Two people meet alone, and one interviews the other by seeking oral responses to oral inquiries. Most interview processes are also sequential. In sequential or serial interview, several persons interview the applicant, in sequence, before a decision is made. In an unstructured sequential interview, each interviewer may ask different questions and form an independent opinion. In a structured sequential interview, each interviewer rates the candidates on a standard evaluation form, using standardized questions. The hiring manager then reviews and compares the evaluations before deciding who to hire A panel interview, also known as a broad interview, is defined as “an interview conducted by a team of interviewers (usually two or three) who interview the candidates simultaneously, and then combine their ratings into the a final panel score. This contrasts with an individual interview in which one interviewer rates one candidate and a serial interview where several interviewers assess a single candidate sequentially. In a serial interview, candidates may cover the same ground the same ground over and over again with each interviewer. The panel format lets interviewers ask follow-up questions based on the candidate’s answers, much as reporters do in press conferences. This may elicit more meaningful responses than are normally produced by a series of one-on-one interviews.

On the other hand, some candidates find panel interviews more stressful so they may actually inhibit responses. An even more stressful variant is the mass interview. Here a panel interviews several candidates simultaneously. The panel poses a problem and then sits back and watches to see which candidate takes the lead in formulating an answer.

It's not clear whether, as a rule, panel interviews are more or less reliable and valid than other types of interviews, because how the employer actually conducts the panel interview has a big effect on reliability and validity. For example, structured panel interviews are more reliable and valid than unstructured ones. Panel interviews in which members use scoring sheets with descriptive scoring anchors (sample answers) are more reliable and valid than those that don't. And training the panel interviewers may boost the interview's reliability, but probably not its validity.

Some interviews are done entirely by telephone. These can actually be more accurate than face- to-face interviews for judging an applicant's conscientiousness, intelligence, and interpersonal skills. Since neither side has to worry about things like clothing nor can handshakes, both parties focus on substantive answers. Or perhaps candidates somewhat surprised by an unexpected call from the recruiter just give more spontaneous answers. In a typical study, interviewers tended to evaluate applicants more favorably in telephone versus face-to-face interviews, particularly where the interviewees were less physically attractive. However the interviewers came to about the same conclusions regarding the interviewees whether the interview was face-to-face or by video conference. The applicants themselves preferred the fact-to-face interviews.

Computerized Interviews:

A computerized selection interview is one in which a job candidate's oral and/or computerized replies are obtained in response to computerized oral, visual, or written questions and/or situation s. Most computerized interviews present the applicant with a series of specific questions regarding his or her background, experience, education, skills, knowledge, and work attitudes that relate to the job for which the person has applied. Other, video-based computerized interviews my also confront candidates with realistic scenarios (such as irate customers) to which they must respond.

Typical computerized interviews present questions in a multiple choice format, one at a time; the applicant is expected to respond to the questions on the screen by pressing a key. Eg: sample interview question for a person applying for a job as a retail store clerk might be:

How would your supervisor rate your customer service skills?

a. Outstanding
b. Above average
c. Average
d. Below average
e. Poor.

II. CONDUCTING AN INTERVIEW EFFICIENTLY

A major step in the interview process is conducting the interview. To conduct the interview effectively is difficult and hence most of the line mangers avoid this task.

The interviewers should take much care in the process of conducting interview in view of the scope for committing mistakes at various levels. Adequate information from the candidate can be obtained by listening to and observing rather talking too much. Further, interviewers very often commit the following mistakes:

- Indulging in discourtesy and rudeness.
- Arriving at conclusions before the interview is over,
- Asking questions mechanically,
- Feeling shyness in asking questions,
- Failing to observe the behavior and tap the unexplored areas.

However, such mistakes by interviewer can be avoided by selecting competent interviewers, training and developing them.

The various sub-activities of conducting the interview are:

- **Open the Interview:**

The interviewer has to open the interview with a conscious effort and with conductive voice, speech and appearance during the first few minutes of the interview. This helps the interviewer to establish a rapport with and gain the confidence of the interviewee.

- Get Complete and Accurate Information:

The interviewer should get full information relating to skill, knowledge, aptitude, attitude, traits of the candidate. The best way of getting full information is by structural interview. The interviewer in order to get complete and accurate information,

- Must be alert for pauses, omissions and diversion of discussion;
- Has to use the language which is clear to the interview;
- Has to ask direct and straight questions in order to avoid ambiguous questions;
- Has to make unjustifiably favorable remarks or unfavorable comments about the applicant's motives or actions with a view to obtain truthful information;
- Has to frame the questions in such a way that the candidate's answer should be elaborate.

- Recording of Observations and impressions:

The interviewer has to record his observation and impressions in the course of interview with a view to manage the information system for evaluating the candidate's suitability at the later stage.

Guiding the interview is essential as,

- To have sufficient discussion (not too much or too less) on a topic;
- To lead the applicant tactfully and surely towards the interview goals;

- Some applicants are talkative and some are intelligent in giving information which they know and in avoiding other areas;
- Applicant sometimes is reticent.

The interviewer has to guide the interview tactfully without causing much psychological inconvenience to the interviewee while aiming at getting complete and reliable information. The next major step of the interview is to check the success of the interviewer in conducting the interview.

The success of the interviewer in conducting the interview can be checked through the following items:

- making favorable impression on the candidate at the beginning of the interview;
- refraining from making judgment at the beginning;
- putting the candidate at ease;
- giving chance for further discussion;
- asking questions at right time, clearly and in appropriate language;
- avoiding unnecessary interference;
- avoiding expression of approval or disapproval of any attitude;
- Talking to a minimum;
- Guiding the interview;
- Obtaining relevant and adequate information.

III. Closing the Interview

Closing of interview is as important as its commencement and it should end pleasantly. The interviewer may show some signs of the close of the interview at an appropriate time interview results should be evaluated after closing the interview.

IV. Evaluation of Interview Results

The interviewer/ the board of interviewers evaluate (s) the candidate's strengths and weakness against the job ad organizational requirements. The evaluation is generally based on the observations, impressions and information collected during the course of interview. However, the final decision about the suitability of candidate to the job is made on the basis of the results of all selection techniques. But the interview results influence the selection decision much more than any other technique. The evaluation may be in descriptive form or grading form or rating form. The interviewer has to strike a fine balance between the job requirements and employee values skills, knowledge etc.

In view of the errors in evaluation, the interviewer has to write explanation of rating on each factor which clarifies his thinking and enables discussion among the interviewers. The interviewer should also take into consideration the educational record, physical attributes, attitudes, sociability and social intelligence, flexibility in behavior, tact, manners, temperament, dependability, self-confidence of the candidate with a view minimize errors in evaluation and to evaluate the candi0date effectively in general.

Qualities of a Successful Interviewer

The interviewer, to be successful should possess the qualities like: elderly outlook, social detachment, intelligence, emotionally matured, interest in understanding human behavior, sociability, active interaction, judgment, expressing the genuine feelings etc. Further, he should be well-educated and trained, should show interest in reading latest literature, equipping himself with latest knowledge and should have thirst for knowledge. He should have thorough understanding of jobs, organization, human behavior, human qualities etc. In addition to the successful interviewer these are some other means to make the interview effective.

Means to Make The Interview Effective:

The interview technique can be used effectively through the following means:

- By selecting the interviewers with higher status, caliber, skill and knowledge;
- Resorting to right type of interview depending upon the situation;
- Studying the background information, data and facts about the candidates before the interview;
- Assessing and evaluating the characteristics and traits of the candidates accurately.
- By basing interview coverage on job and organizational requirements;
- Following time management techniques to collect as much important information as possible within the available time;
- Checking beforehand the reliability and validity of the interview and method;
- Respecting interviewee's interest and individuality;
- Clearly informing the interviewee the purpose of the interview;
- Making the interviewee feel at ease throughout the interview;
- Encouraging interviewee to speak freely;
- Interviewer should try to understand the words used by the interviewees;
- Interviewers should not have personal views and opinions.

WORK SAMPLES

Experts consider work samples and simulations such as the assessment centers tests. However, they differ from most tests because they measure job performance directly. With video-based situational tests, for example, examines the candidates with situations representative of the job for which they're applying and evaluate their responses to these hypothetical situations.

Work Sampling For Employee Selection:

The work sampling technique measures how a candidate actually performs some of the job's basic tasks. This has several advantages. It measures actual on-the-job tasks, so it's harder for applicants to fake answers. Work samples more clearly relate to the job a candidate is getting tested for, so in terms of fairness and fair employment, he may be on safer ground. The work sample's content, the actual tasks the person must perform is not as likely to be unfair to minorities as might a personnel test that possibly emphasized middle class concepts and values. Work sampling does not delve into the applicant's personality or psyche, so there's almost no chance of it being viewed as an invasion of privacy. Designed properly, work sampling tests also exhibit better validity than do other tests designed to predict performance.

The basic procedure is to choose several tasks crucial to performing the job and to test applicants on samples of each. An observer monitors performance on each task, and indicates on a checklist how well the applicant performs. Here is an example. In developing a work sampling test for maintenance mechanics experts first listed all possible job tasks like "install pulleys and belts" and "install and align a motor". Four crucial tasks were installing pulleys and belts, disassembling and installing a gearbox, installing and aligning a motor and pressing a bushing into a sprocket.

They then broke down these four tasks into the steps required to complete them. Mechanics could perform each step in a slightly different way, of course. Since some approaches were better than others, the experts gave a different weight to different approaches.

One of the steps required for installing pulleys and belts "checks key before installing." Possible approaches include checking the key against (1) the shaft, (2) the pulley, or (3) neither. The scores reflecting the worth of each method is listed out. The applicant performs the task, and the observer checks off the approach used.

A management assessment center is a two to three day simulation in which 10 to 12 candidates perform realistic management tasks (like making presentations) under the observation of experts

who appraise each candidate's leadership potential. The center itself may be a plain conference room, but it is often a special room with a one-way mirror to facilitate observation. Typical simulated exercises include:

The in-basket: These exercises confront the candidate with an accumulation of reports, memos, notes of incoming phone calls, letters, and other materials collected in the actual or computerized in-basket of the simulated job he or she is about to start. The candidate must take appropriate action on each item. Trained evaluators then review thc candidate's efforts.

Leaderless group discussion: Trainers give a leaderless group a discussion question and tell

members to arrive at a group decision. They then evaluate each group member's interpersonal skills, acceptance by the group, leadership ability, and individual influence.

Management Games: Participants solve realistic problems as members of simulated companies competing in a marketplace. They may have to decide, for instance, how to advertise and manufacture, and how much inventory to stock.

Individual presentation: Trainers evaluate each participant's communication skills and persuasiveness by having each make an assigned oral presentation

Objective tests: A center typically includes tests of personality, mental ability, interests, and achievements.

The Interview: Most require an interview between employer's panel, observer and each

participant to assess the latter's interests, past performance, and motivation. And this concludes the final selection process. Recruiting then depends upon post interview assessment of the concerned.

CHAPTER TWO

PERFORMANCE APPRAISAL

Appraisal is both inevitable and universal. In the absence of a carefully structured system of appraisal, people will tend to judge the work performance of others, including subordinates, naturally, informally and arbitrarily. The human inclination to judge can create serious motivational, ethical and legal problems in the workplace. Without a structured appraisal system, there is little chance of ensuring that the judgements made will be lawful, fair, defensible and accurate.

Performance appraisal systems began as simple methods of income justification. That is, appraisal was used to decide whether or not the salary or wage of an individual employee was justified. The process was firmly linked to material outcomes. If an employee's performance was found to be less than ideal, a cut in pay would follow. On the other hand, if their performance was better than the supervisor expected, a pay rise was in order. Sometimes this basic system succeeded in getting the results that were intended; but more often than not, it failed.

These observations were confirmed in empirical studies. Pay rates were important, yes; but they were not the only element that had an impact on employee performance. It was found that other issues, such as morale and self-esteem, could also have a major influence.

As a result, the traditional emphasis on reward outcomes was progressively rejected. In the 1950s in the United States, the potential usefulness of appraisal as tool for motivation and development was gradually recognized. The general model of performance appraisal, as it is known today, began from that time.

Performance appraisal may be defined as a structured formal interaction between a subordinate and supervisor, that usually takes the form of a periodic interview (annual or semi-annual), in which the work performance of the subordinate is examined and discussed, with a view to identifying weaknesses and strengths as well as opportunities for improvement and skills development.

In many organizations - but not all - appraisal results are used, either directly or indirectly, to help determine reward outcomes. That is, the appraisal results are used to identify the better performing employees who should get the majority of available merit pay increases, bonuses, and promotions.

By the same token, appraisal results are used to identify the poorer performers who may require some form of counseling, or in extreme cases, demotion, dismissal or decreases in pay. (Organizations need to be awarc of laws in their country that might restrict their capacity to dismiss employees or decrease pay.)

Whether this is an appropriate use of performance appraisal - the assignment and justification of rewards and penalties - is a very uncertain and contentious matter.

Basic Purposes

Effective performance appraisal systems contain two basic systems operating in conjunction: an evaluation systcm and a feedback system.

The main aim of the evaluation system is to identify the performance gap (if any). This gap is the shortfall that occurs when performance does not meet the standard set by the organization as acceptable.

The main aim of the feedback system is to inform the employee about the quality of his or her performance. (However, the information flow is not exclusively one way. The appraisers also

receives feedback from the employee about job problems, etc.)

One of the best ways to appreciate the purposes of performance appraisal is to look at it from the different viewpoints of the main stakeholders: the employee and the organization.

BENEFITS OF APPRAISAL

Perhaps the most significant benefit of appraisal is that, in the rush and bustle of daily working life, it offers a rare chance for a supervisor and subordinate to have "time out" for a one-on-one discussion of important work issues that might not otherwise be addressed.

Almost universally, where performance appraisal is conducted properly, both supervisors and subordinates have reported the experience as beneficial and positive.

Appraisal offers a valuable opportunity to focus on work activities and goals, to identify and correct existing problems, and to encourage better future performance. Thus the performance of the whole organization is enhanced.

For many employees, an "official" appraisal interview may be the only time they get to have exclusive, uninterrupted access to their supervisor. Said one employee of a large organization after his first formal performance appraisal, "In twenty years of work, that's the first time anyone has ever bothered to sit down and tell me how I'm doing."

The value of this intense and purposeful interaction between a supervisors and subordinate should not be underestimated.

Motivation and Satisfaction

Performance appraisal can have a profound effect on levels of employee motivation and satisfaction - for better as well as for worse.

Performance appraisal provides employees with recognition for their work efforts. The power of social recognition as an incentive has been long noted. In fact, there is evidence that human beings will even prefer negative recognition in preference to no recognition at all.

If nothing else, the existence of an appraisal program indicates to an employee that the organization is genuinely interested in their individual performance and development. This alone can have a positive influence on the individual's sense of worth, commitment and belonging.

The strength and prevalence of this natural human desire for individual recognition should not be overlooked. Absenteeism and turnover rates in some organizations might be greatly reduced if more attention were paid to it. Regular performance appraisal, at least, is a good start.

Training and Development

Performance appraisal offers an excellent opportunity - perhaps the best that will ever occur - for a supervisor and subordinate to recognize and agree upon individual training and development needs.

During the discussion of an employee's work performance, the presence or absence of work skills can become very obvious - even to those who habitually reject the idea of training for them!

Performance appraisal can make the need for training more pressing and relevant by linking it clearly to performance outcomes and future career aspirations.

From the point of view of the organization as a whole, consolidated appraisal data can form a picture of the overall demand for training. This data may be analysed by variables such as sex, department, etc. It can provide an efficient training needs audit for the entire organization.

Recruitment and Induction

Appraisal data can be used to monitor the success of the organization's recruitment and induction practices. For example, how well are the employees performing who were hired in the past two years?

Appraisal data can also be used to monitor the effectiveness of changes in recruitment strategies. By following the yearly data related to new hires (and given sufficient numbers on which to base the analysis) it is possible to assess whether the general quality of the workforce is improving, staying steady, or declining.

Employee Evaluation

Though often understated or even denied, evaluation is a legitimate and major objective of performance appraisal. But the need to evaluate (i.e., to judge) is also an ongoing source of tension, since evaluative and developmental priorities appear to frequently clash. Yet at its most basic level, performance appraisal is the process of examining and evaluating the performance of an individual.

Though organizations have a clear right - some would say a duty - to conduct such evaluations of performance, many still recoil from the idea. To them, the explicit process of judgement can be dehumanizing and demoralizing and a source of anxiety and distress to employees.

It is been said by some that appraisal cannot serve the needs of evaluation and development at the same time; it must be one or the other.

But there may be an acceptable middle ground, where the need to evaluate employees objectively, and the need to encourage and develop them, can be balanced.

KEY POINTS TO REMEMBER

i. **Document Everything:**

In a good formal appraisal system everything should be written down. A good performance appraisal system should allow for providing supporting documentation so that when action is taken based on the appraisal, the fairness and relevance of the appraisal can be scrutinized and the entire process made transparent. There is already a lot of literature on how to develop a sound performance appraisal system and HR managers would do well to study them before launching any new system.

v. Set Clear Goals:

The key idea behind a good performance evaluation system is to reward rather than punish or meet legal requirements, help to lay down & communicate clear performance goals and measure progress, help identify laggards & whether they need any specific help in terms of training and mentoring that can enable them to improve, help identify bosses who are stifling talent or are in some way or the other standing in the way of better realization of an

employee's potential & on the whole lay down a solid channel of communication between employees & the top management. A good appraisal system should take care of all these goals.

v. Make the Process User-Friendly:

The appraisal system should be simple, easy to understand and easy to use. Since a good appraisal system almost always require a participatory approach on the part of the boss and his subordinates, the paper work should be kept to a minimum and as simple as possible. A basic and standardized form is highly recommended as it would enable an open, transparent and uniform appraisal process for all employees. To take care of specific needs of specific departments, standardized forms for particular departments may be necessary.

v. Allow for Flexibility:

Standardized forms and a uniform system can lead to too much rigidity. Hence, allow for flexibility even within the uniform format. This may be especially relevant in small businesses where one person may have several unique competencies and may be looking after several different functions of different types. Have a system that can take care of such situations so that even as it allows flexibility, it also minimizes the risk of arbitrariness.

v. Make it Participatory:

A good appraisal system always allows employees to participate in the review process. Employees must be allowed to give their own self-appraisals by giving them an opportunity in the appraisal form to list their own strengths, weaknesses and goals for the coming year. During the review compare notes and finally try to come up, as often as possible, with an appraisal that has the employee's consent.

v. Set Achieable Goals:

If you own a business it is likely that you will work night and day or for that matter do whatever it takes to make the business successful. But you can hardly expect your employees to have a similar attitude, although there are people who do show as much commitment. So be realistic and set such goals that are achievable. Try to customize goals to individual employees so that each have a realistic chance of meeting those goals. Nothing motivates an employee more than being able to meet goals and being recognized for the success. Goals that are too tough and which most are almost sure to fail to meet can only help to demoralize your staff instead of egging them on to raise their levels of performance. Instead if you raise the bar gradually and in a way such that more people succeed in meeting those goals than fail, over a period of time you will be surprised to find how much people have progressed.

v. **Adjust your Business Plan:** A well-designed and well-executed performance appraisal process will enable you and your staff to arrive at clear and achievable goals that both you and your staff have agreed to achieve. Adjust your business plan accordingly so that the performance review should end up with giving you a far more workable business plan which will, more often than not, succeed while helping to retain talent by keeping employees satisfied.

PERFORMANCE EVALUATION TIPS FOR SUPERVISORS

- Be honest and fair in evaluating all employees. Be certain that you as the supervisor have reviewed all of your employees in an objective and consistent manner as individuals and relative to other employees in the group. The purpose of performance evaluations is to take a realistic snapshot of the employee's performance. Don't say the employee is improving if (s)he is not performing well.
- Be consistent in your approach. Don't create a situation where it appears that you create excuses for one employee while holding another employee accountable. Define your criteria for each level of ranking and use the same criteria for every employee. Don't set separate criteria for certain employees.
- Give your comments. A ranking or number used to rank an employee's performance is useless without a written comment. Comments are required for any ranking that is less than "3 or meets expectations" or rated "5 or superior." Comments may confirm achievements or be constructive depending on the nature of the ranking.
- Make your comments consistent with the rankings. Don't give someone a "meets expectations" ranking if your comment describes a substandard performance.
- Be realistic. Don't inflate ratings. It only inflates an employee's expectations.

- Rate the employee's performance, not the employee's "attitude." Keep your comments job related and based on the employee's ability to perform his/her job. Avoid phrases like "bad attitude," "he's not a team player," and other subjective type comments. Explain the behavior that is a result of the "attitude."

- Set goals with the employee. Don't just criticize a deficient performer; set goals for follow up and for improvement or development. Work together to create a plan of action to help the employee in deficient areas and to establish goals for the coming year. Set a follow up period and be sure to reevaluate the employee at the appropriate time.
- A performance evaluation should motivate an employee to want to improve. The employee should feel excited about the challenges and his/her ability to meet them. If employees hear only about their failures and weaknesses, they'll start to believe they can't succeed. If employees get support and encouragement from their supervisor, they'll gain the desire and confidence to keep trying. When the supervisors' suggestions for improvement bring results - and recognition - employees are even more likely to listen to future suggestions.
- There should be no surprises. The evaluation should be a review of the past year's performance. Through previous counseling and other communications, the employee should be aware of any concerns you might have about their job performance. The annual evaluation should not be the first time the employee learns of your concerns.
- One tool that may be used is to ask the employee to review his or her own performance and expectations for the future by preparing a self-appraisal. They may complete the same evaluation form that the supervisor uses or may draft a memo or list reviewing performance strengths and weaknesses and future goals. Having the employee go through the same exercise may make it easier for him or her to understand the value of the evaluation process.

PERFORMANCE REVIEW

Performance Review is an annual process that formally documents performance and identifies ways to help employees continue to contribute to achieving the company's mission and to provide staff with personal and professional growth opportunities.

There are essentially two components to this program:

- ***Look Back***

Reviewing the past year, discussing how the employee performed and giving constructive feedback

- ***Look Ahead***

Identifying specific ways in which the employee could improve performance, build skills and competencies, and/or take on additional responsibilities and setting goals and objectives for the coming year.

Coaching & managing your staff in all the on-going activities, whereas the formal performance review occurs once a year. If you and your staff have been communicating clearly and effectively throughout the year, there should be no surprises at the performance review meeting.

Setting Goals and Objectives

The basic criteria for the evaluation centers around the supervisor and employee having discussed and established *appropriate* goals and objectives relative to the performance of the specific job. If this discussion has not occurred, then it should take place as soon as possible.

The employee must clearly understand the responsibilities of the position, the expectations that the supervisor has, and the goals that are to be achieved. In establishing goals it is again important to seek the full potential of the individual, not merely to allow "business as usual" to set the standard for the identification of goals. The supervisor and employee should discuss the goals and the supervisor should encourage a visionary attitude in this process and establish goals that stretch the employee's abilities to continually improve both in terms of the individual's own performance and the services provided.

When you meet with each member of your staff individually at the end of the year, you will talk about several things:

- How the employee performed his/her major job responsibilities,
- The Skill and Competency Model for support staff to identify any major changes to the skill or competency levels since the prior year, and
- The actions the employee can take to maintain or further develop his/her skills, knowledge and competencies, and, if necessary, improve performance.
- In addition to the annual performance review, we suggest also meeting on an informal basis mid-year to see how things are going. This is particularly important if there has been a history of performance problems or if you and your staff don't have much opportunity to communicate regularly during the normal course of activities.
- Regular and frequent discussion is needed between supervisor and employee on the status of work being done, what is and is not being accomplished, what factors affect the work, and what is the quality of the work performed. By providing regular feedback and discussing the issues throughout the year, the supervisor minimizes anxiety levels at the time of the "formal" evaluation, since the assessment should basically be known to the employee already. It is important that the supervisor and the employee continue to understand the priorities and expectations as they change throughout the year. It is also important for the supervisor to be fully aware of the actual work being done and the impact of that work, through direct observation and, when appropriate, through obtaining the input from others.

Some of the items to think about are:

- Is the employee performing at expected levels? Have you clearly expressed your expectations?
- Has anything occurred that might change those expectations or the employee's ability to meet those expectations, such as a change in the department, new technology, etc?

- Is there anything that should be handled differently to help the employee be successful in his/her job?
- The goal is to keep the lines of communication open so that there are no surprises at the end of the year, and to change inappropriate behavior before it escalates or becomes entrenched.
- Performance management is designed to help employees take ownership for their own performance and career growth. Employees will complete a self-review and are encouraged to actively participate in the review discussion. This not only gives you insight into the employee's perspective, but gives him/her an active, rather than passive, role in the process of his/her own career progression.
- You will also complete a review of the employee's performance. At the review meeting, you and the employee will compare and discuss the two reviews. You may want to include Human Resources if you feel you need a facilitator in reaching consensus.
- It is important to remember that this process is not designed for you to relinquish your supervisory responsibilities. Rather it is designed to facilitate communications and discussion. Ultimately, the goal is to help the employee
- Accomplish the necessary job responsibilities,
- Work in a way that is consistent with the broader objectives of the department and the company,
- Receive appropriate guidance and be given accurate, regular and constructive feedback, and
- Identify promotional opportunities, if applicable.

TIPS FOR CONDUCTING THE REVIEW MEETING

- The tone of the review meeting is just as important as the content. The goal is to have a productive meeting about job performance and developmental activities; the meeting should not be adversarial. Here are some tips to help make the meeting more successful:
- Set a mutually convenient meeting time and reserve about 1 hour. Neither of you should feel rushed.
- Select a private room and create a comfortable non-threatening environment; establish a warm, friendly and supportive tone; ensure that

outside interruptions are avoided.

- Encourage two-way conversation; avoid monologues; encourage the employee to make comments; use open-ended questions and listen attentively.
- When giving feedback, be clear and to the point, drawing on comments and examples you have written on the review form.
- Reinforce good performance by referencing specific examples and calling attention to the actions you would like to see continue.
- Remain objective and non-judgmental by focusing on performance relative to establishing expectations rather than on personality; do not compare the individual to specific coworkers.
- Overall, you want to show your interest in the employee's performance, development and commitment to achievement.

Ideally, you and your employee should have a chance to look over both reviews before the meeting. Some people, however, may feel more comfortable sharing the reviews at the meeting. After the review, make a copy for the employee and yourself. The original should be sent to the appropriate Department Head for his or her signature. A final, signed copy should be sent to Human Resources for placement in the employee's file.

COMPLETING THE FORM

The evaluation form itself is to be used as a tool in helping the supervisor and the employee to think about the performance of the job and to assess that performance against the expectations and goals that were established. The employee should complete the Self-Assessment or Self Review separately and provide the supervisor with a copy. The supervisor and employee MUST meet and discuss the evaluation before it is finalized.

The Performance Review should address performance over time. Don't focus on isolated incidents unless they represent a pattern of behavior. On the other hand, recent changes in performance, either positive or negative, should be acknowledged and discussed.

It is important that the employee's review be clear and accurate. People should know where they stand and understand how you, as their supervisor, perceive their performance. Additionally, if the employee is not performing adequately, it is important to clearly and specifically document the performance to establish a history in the event that the employee is terminated.

Each year, the employee should develop specific plans to maintain and improve skills, knowledge and competencies. You should discuss those plans and how they address any identified areas for improvement.

When conducting a review, it is important to consider the efforts made to discuss the completion of any development action plans made in the prior year. While these are not actually part of the performance review, they are an indicator of the employee's interest in improving and growing. This is particularly important when the action plans involved "remedial" work to bring performance up to a satisfactory level.

APPRAISAL METHODS

In a landmark study, Locher & Teel (1977) found that the three most common appraisal methods in general use are rating scales (56%), essay methods (25%) and results- oriented or MBO methods (13%). For a description of each, follow the button links on the left.

Certain techniques in performance appraisal have been thoroughly investigated, and some have been found to yield better results than others.

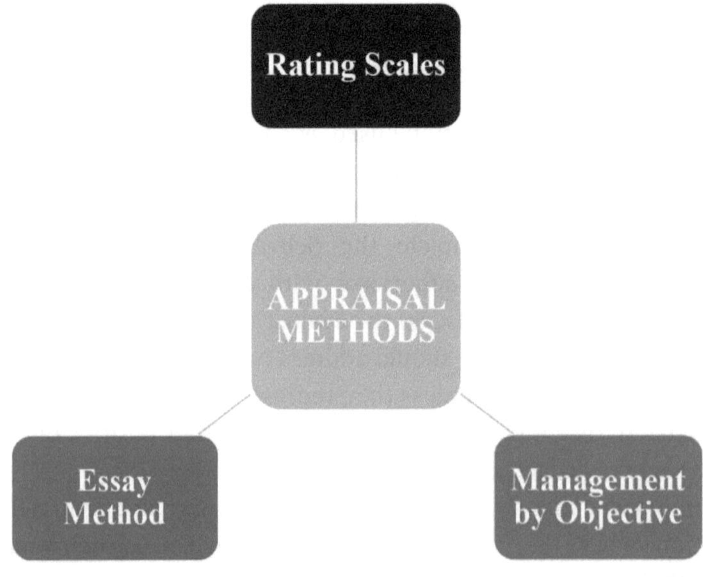

1. RATING SCALES

The rating scale method offers a high degree of structure for appraisals. Each employee trait or characteristic is rated on a bipolar scale that usually has several points ranging from "poor" to "excellent" (or some similar arrangement).

The traits assessed on these scales include employee attributes such as cooperation, communications ability, initiative, punctuality and technical (work skills) competence. The nature and scope of the traits selected for inclusion is limited only by the imagination of the scale's designer, or by the organization's need to know.

The one major provision in selecting traits is that they should be in some way relevant to the appraisee's job. The traits selected by some organizations have been unwise and have resulted in legal action on the grounds of discrimination.

Advantages:

- The greatest advantage of rating scales is that they are structured and standardised. This allows ratings to be easily compared and contrasted - even for entire workforces.
- Each employee is subjected to the same basic appraisal process and rating criteria, with the same range of responses. This encourages equality in treatment for all appraisees and imposes standard measures of performance across all parts of the organization.
- Easy to use and understand.
- The concept of the rating scale makes obvious sense; both appraisers and appraisees have an intuitive appreciation for the simple and efficient logic of the bipolar scale. The result is widespread acceptance and popularity for this approach.

Disadvantages:

- Trait Relevance: are the selected rating-scale traits clearly relevant to the jobs of all the appraisees? It is inevitable that with a standardised and fixed system of appraisal that certain traits will have a greater relevance in some jobs than in others. The relevance of rating scales is therefore said to be context-sensitive. Job and workplace circumstances must be taken into account.

- Systemic Disadvantage: Rating scales, and the traits they purport to measure, generally attempt to encapsulate all the relevant indicators of employee performance. There is an assumption that all the true and best indicators of performance are included, and all false and irrelevant indicators are excluded. This assumption very difficult to prove in practice. It is possible that an employee's performance may depend on factors that have not been included in the selected traits. Such employees may end up with ratings that do not truly or fairly reflect their effort or value to the organization.

- Perceived Meaning: Problems of perceived meaning occur when appraisers do not share the same opinion about the meaning of the selected traits and the language used on the rating scales. Eg: to one appraiser, an employee may demonstrate the trait of initiative by reporting work problems to a supervisor. To another appraiser, this might suggest an excessive dependence on supervisory assistance - and thus a lack of initiative. As well, the language and terms used to construct a scale - such as "Performance exceeds expectations" or "Below average skill" - may mean different things to different appraisers.

- Rating Errors: The problem here is not so much errors in perception as errors in appraiser judgement and motive. Unlike perceptual errors, these errors may be (at times) deliberate. The most common rating error is central tendency. Busy appraisers, or those wary of confrontations and repercussions, may be tempted to dole out too many passive, middle-of-the-road ratings (e.g., "satisfactory" or "adequate"), regardless of the actual performance of a subordinate. Thus the spread of ratings tends to clump excessively around the middle of the scale. This problem is worsened in organizations where the appraisal process does not enjoy strong management support, or where the appraisers do not feel confident with the task of appraisal.

1. ESSAY METHOD

In the essay method approach, the appraiser prepares a written statement about the employee being appraised.

The statement usually concentrates on describing specific strengths and weaknesses in job performance. It also suggests courses of action to remedy the identified problem areas.

The statement may be written and edited by the appraiser alone, or it be composed in collaboration with the appraisee.

Advantages:

- The essay method is far less structured and confining than the rating scale method. It permits the appraiser to examine almost any relevant issue or attribute of performance. This contrasts sharply with methods where the appraisal criteria are rigidly defined.
- Appraisers may place whatever degree of emphasis on issues or attributes that they feel appropriate. Thus the process is open-ended and very flexible.
- The appraiser is not locked into an appraisal system the limits expression or assumes that employee traits can be neatly dissected and scaled.

Disadvantages:

- Essay methods are time-consuming and difficult to administer. Appraisers often find the essay technique more demanding than methods such as rating scales.
- The techniques greatest advantage - freedom of expression - is also its greatest handicap. The varying writing skills of appraisers can upset and distort the whole process.
- The process is subjective and, in consequence, it is difficult to compare and contrast the results of individuals or to draw any broad

conclusions about organizational needs.

3. RESULTS METHOD: MANAGEMENT BY OBJECTIVES (MBO)

The use of management objectives was first widely advocated in the 1950s by the noted management theorist Peter Drucker.

MBO (management by objectives) methods of performance appraisal are results-oriented. That is, they seek to measure employee performance by examining the extent to which predetermined work objectives have been met.

Usually the objectives are established jointly by the supervisor and subordinate. An example of an objective for a sales manager might be: Increase the gross monthly sales volume to $250,000 by 30 June.

Once an objective is agreed, the employee is usually expected to self-audit; that is, to identify the skills needed to achieve the objective. Typically they do not rely on others to locate and specify their strengths and weaknesses. They are expected to monitor their own development and progress.

Advantages:

- The MBO approach overcomes some of the problems that arise as a result of assuming that the employee traits needed for job success can be reliably identified and measured. Instead of assuming traits, the MBO method concentrates on actual outcomes.

If the employee meets or exceeds the set objectives, then he or she has demonstrated an acceptable level of job performance. Employees are judged according to real outcomes, and not on their potential for success, or on someone's subjective opinion of their abilities.

- The guiding principle of the MBO approach is that direct results can be observed,

whereas the traits and attributes of employees (which may or may not contribute to performance) must be guessed at or inferred.

- The MBO method recognizes the fact that it is difficult to neatly dissect all the complex and varied elements that go to make up employee performance.
- MBO advocates claim that the performance of employees cannot be broken up into so many constituent parts - as one might take apart an engine to study it. But put all the parts together and the performance may be directly observed and measured.

Disadvantages:

- MBO methods of performance appraisal can give employees a satisfying sense of autonomy and achievement. But on the downside, they can lead to unrealistic expectations about what can and cannot be reasonably accomplished.
- Supervisors and subordinates must have very good "reality checking" skills to use MBO appraisal methods. They will need these skills during the initial stage of objective setting, and for the purposes of self-auditing and self-monitoring.
- Unfortunately, research studies have shown repeatedly that human beings tend to lack the skills needed to do their own "reality checking". Nor are these skills easily conveyed by training. Reality itself is an intensely personal experience, prone to all forms of perceptual bias.
- One of the strengths of the MBO method is the clarity of purpose that flows from a set of well-articulated objectives. But this can be a source of weakness also. It has become very apparent that the modern organization must be flexible to survive. Objectives, by their very nature, tend to impose a certain rigidity.
- It is also possible that fluid objectives may be distorted to disguise or justify failures in performance.

ISSUES IN PERFORMANCE APPRAISAL

The problem with subjective measure is the rating which is not verifiable by others and has the opportunity for bias. The rate biases include:

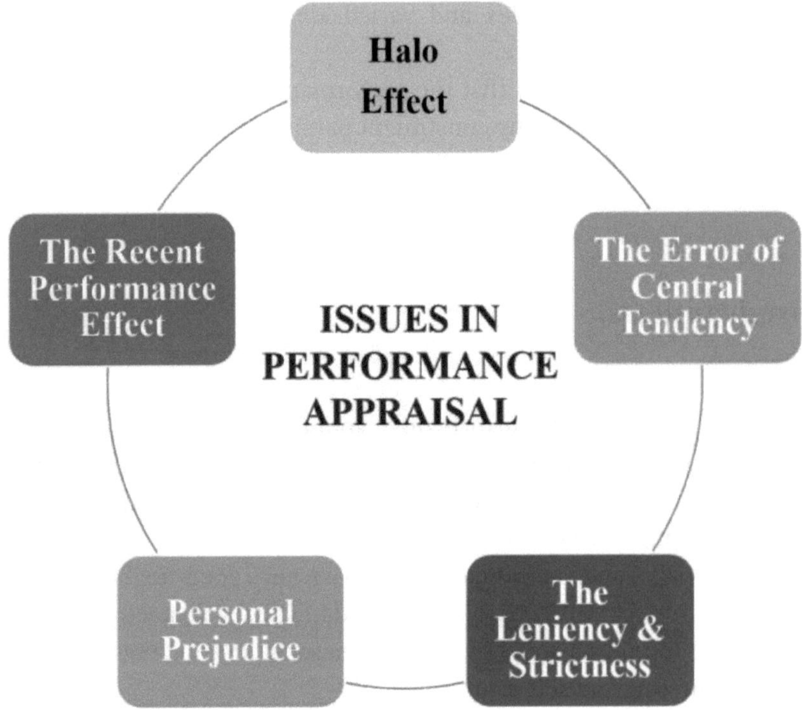

a. **Halo Effect:** It is the tendency of the raters to depend excessively on the rating of one trait or behavioral consideration in rating all others traits or behavioral considerations. One way of minimizing the halo effect is appraising all the employees by one trait before going to rate on the basis of another trait.

b. **The error of Central Tendency:** Some raters follow play safe policy in rating by rating all the employees around the middle point of the rating scale and they avoid rating the people at both the extremes of the scale. They follow play safe policy because of answerability to management or lack of knowledge about the job and person he is rating or least interest in his job.

c. **The Leniency and Strictness:** The leniency bias crops when some raters have a tendency to be liberal in their rating by assigning higher rates consistently. Such ratings do not serve any purpose. Equally damaging one is assigning consistently low rates.

d. **Personal Prejudice:** If the rater dislikes any employee or any group, he may rate them at the lower end, which may distort the rating purpose and affect the career of these employees.

e. **The Recent Performance Effect:** The raters generally remember the recent actions, of the employee at the time of rating and rate on the basis of these recent actions favorable or unfavorable than on the whole activities.

Other factors that are considered as problems in Performance Appraisal are:

- Failure of the superiors in conducting performance appraisal and post-performance appraisal interview.
- Most part of the appraisal is based on subjectivity.
- Less reliability and validity of the performance appraisal techniques.
- Negative ratings affect interpersonal relations and industrial relations system.
- Influence of external environmental factors and uncontrollable internal factors.
- Feedback and post appraisal interview may have a setback on production.
- Management emphasizes on punishment rather than development of an employee in performance appraisal.
- Some ratings particularly about the potential appraisal are purely based on guess work.

The other problems of performance appraisal reported by various studies are:

- Relationship between appraisal rates and performances after promotions was not significant.
- Some superiors completed appraisal reports within a few minutes.
- Absence of inter-rater reliability.
- The situation was unpleasant in feedback interview.
- Superiors lack that tact of offering the suggestions constructively to subordinates.
- Supervisors were often confused due to too many objectives of performance appraisal.

Advantages of Performance Appraisal through Computers:

There will be an objective analysis of traits of both the superior and subordinate and a chance to subordinate to express his views even after performance appraisal.

An employee shall express his emotional needs and his value system which may not be possible direct face to face with superior. Communication through computer overcomes the communication barrier between the superior and subordinate.

Computer based appraisal will remove the inherent weakness of the appraisal system that is subjective assessment of vague and abstract performance targets, unclear guidelines for appraisal etc.

CHAPTER THREE

MANPOWER PLANNING

Under staffing loses the business economies of scale and specialization, orders, customers and profits.

Over staffing is wasteful and expensive, if sustained, and it is costly to eliminate because of modern legislation in respect of redundancy payments, consultation, minimum periods of notice, etc. Very importantly, over staffing reduces the competitive efficiency of the business.

Planning staff levels requires that an assessment of present and future needs of the organization be compared with present resources and future predicted resources. Appropriate steps then be planned to bring demand and supply into balance.

Manpower Planning is the process of deciding what are the various openings available in the company and how they need to be filled. It takes care of all of the company's present and future vacancies – right from the front office staff to the clerks till the President and the CEO.

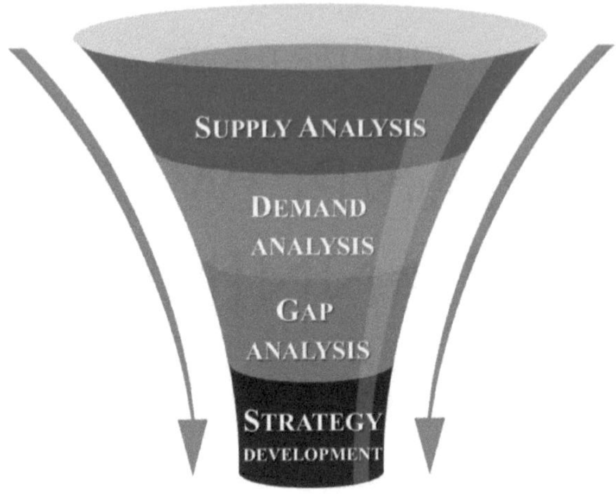

Thus the first step is to take a 'satellite picture' of the existing workforce profile (numbers, skills, ages, flexibility, gender, experience, forecast capabilities, character, potential, etc. of existing employees) and then to adjust this for 1, 3 and 10 years ahead by amendments for normal turnover, planned staff movements, retirements, etc., in line with the business plan for the corresponding time frames.

DEFINITION AND IMPORTANCE OF MANPOWER PLANNING

Planning is nothing but using the available assets for the effective implementation of the production plans. After the preparing the plans, people are grouped together to achieve organizational objectives.

Planning is concerned with coordinating, motivating and controlling of the various activities within the organization. Time required for acquiring the material, capital and machinery should be taken into account. Manager has to reasonably predict future events and plan out the production. The basic purpose of the management is to increase the production, so that the profit margin can be increased. Manager has to guess the future business and to take timely and correct decisions in respect of company objectives, policies and cost performances. The plans need to be supported by all the members of the organization. Planning is making a decision in advance what is to be done. It is the willpower of course of action to achieve the desired results. It is a kind of future picture where events are sketched. It can be defined as a mental process requiring the use of intellectual faculty, imagination, foresight and sound judgment.

It involves problem solving and decision making. Management has to prepare for short term strategy and measure the achievements, while the long term plans are prepared to develop the better and new products, services, expansion to keep the interest of the owners.

Advantages of Manpower Planning:

Manpower planning ensures optimum use of available human resources.

1. It is useful both for organization and nation.
2. It generates facilities to educate people in the organization.
3. It brings about fast economic developments.
4. It boosts the geographical mobility of labor.
5. It provides smooth working even after expansion of the organization.
6. It opens possibility for workers for future promotions, thus providing incentive.
7. It creates healthy atmosphere of encouragement and motivation in the organization.
8. It provides help for career development of the employees.

Steps in Manpower Planning

1. Predict manpower plans
2. Design job description and the job requirements
3. Find adequate sources of recruitment.
4. Give boost to youngsters by appointment to higher posts.
5. Best motivation for internal promotion.
6. Look after the expected losses due to retirement, transfer and other issues.
7. See for replacement due to accident, death, dismissals and promotion.

Factors which affect the Efficiency of Labor:

1. Inheritance: Persons from good collection are bound to work professionally. The quality and rate of physical as well as mental development, which is dissimilar in case of different individuals is the result of genetic differences.
2. Climate: Climatic location has a definite effect on the efficiency of the workers.
3. Health of worker: worker's physical condition plays a very important part in performing the work. Good health means the sound mind, in the sound body.
4. Personal qualities: persons with dissimilar personal qualities bound to have definite differences in their behaviour and methods of working. The personal qualities influence the quality of work.
5. Wages: proper wages guarantees certain reasons in standard of living, such as cheerfulness, discipline etc. and keep workers satisfy. This provides incentive to work.
6. Hours of work: long and tiring hours of work exercise have bad effect on the competence of the workers.

Downsizing of Manpower:

Downsizing of manpower gives the correct picture about the number of people to be employed to complete given task in the predetermined period. It is used for achieving fundamental growth in the concern. It can work out the correct price by the resource building or capacity building. It aims at correct place, correct man on a correct job.

CHAPTER FOUR

Career Development & Successio Planning

Career development is the process of becoming aware of the opportunities available, the constraints and consequences of a career choice, identifying career-related goals and working towards attainment of such goals.

Succession planning is the process of having the right number and the right type of people at the right places and time doing things which result in long-term benefits for both the organisation and the individual.

The basic unit of both career development and succession planning is the employee. The organisation's objective in implementing career development and succession planning is similar

- having available the right type of individuals through all phases of the organisation's development in order to achieve the corporate objectives.

As individuals develop, they would tend to leave if they do not see opportunities for career growth within the organisation. If there is no succession planning, or if there is poor communication regarding the opportunities available within the organisation, the individual may choose to leave and the organisation subsequently loses out. As far as the organisation is concerned, the availability of a structure to assist individuals achieve their career goals would be useless unless this is tied to Succession Planning.

Since the individual's career plans do not necessarily have to revolve around his or her present organisation, it is important for the latter to match both the individual's career goals and that of the company so that both are moving in the same direction.

Responsibility for career development should be jointly held by both the organisation's top management and the individual. The organisation's duty is to provide the opportunities for career development and it is then up to the individual to take advantage of those opportunities. The organisation should also ensure that its employees are aware of such and now how to make use of these opportunities. If after all such opportunities are made available and the individual does not show any interest, then there is nothing the organisation can do.

Where succession planning is concerned, however, it is solely the responsibility of the senior management to ensure that there are second liners for each important position in the organisation. These second liners should be available, trained and ready to assume those positions of higher responsibility if and when they become vacant. Without this back-up system, the organisation may face tremendous loss in the event of any untimely vacancy due to resignation, prolonged illness or death.

The starting point should be succession planning to ensure that all-important portions like technical or professional specialists and all senior and middle managers have back-ups. The human resource manager is usually assigned the responsibility of coordinating the system. He

should have a clear understanding of the present manpower situation and the organisation's operational objectives in regard to:

- Capital investments
- Product changes, additions, deletions

- Changes in raw materials and processes

The above information is usually part of the human resource plan, and if available for periods of from one to five years, will give an indication of future requirements for the positions for which succession planning is required. A decision should be made in terms of which are the key positions needing back-ups so that projections of future requirements can be made. Projections for period over five years would be too inaccurate to be of any real use especially in an ever- changing environment. Once the positions have been identified, historical data relating to turnover, retirements, promotions, transfers and terminations need to be considered.

Having identified what the human resource requirements are, the human resource manager should now re-examine what is available within the organisation and this is best accomplished through a skills inventory or skills bank system. With this system, the organisation would have a complete picture of what each employee is capable of doing.

Also useful in the systematic analysis of employees is the use of data from annual performance appraisals, although at times there may be doubts as to the accuracy of the evaluations. Another alternative source of employee strengths and weaknesses is through the use of assessment centres.

Once all the available data has been obtained, succession charts can be prepared. For each key position the chart should show the name and age of the present incumbent and the names of all possible replacements. Information regarding the readiness and suitability of the potential replacements can then be entered so that should any vacancies arise, senior management can see at a glance who are those from within who are capable of filling the position.

When a vacancy occurs, decisions as to whether to promote from within and hire a replacement from outside are obviously not within the sole discretion of the human resource manager. He can make his recommendations but the top management must make the decision. With a succession planning system installed, however, such decisions will already have been made.

Career development is a shared responsibility between the individuals in a company and the organisation where the latter provides the opportunities and the employees undertake the personal improvements to achieve their career plans. In some organisations which are committed to career development, all employees are expected and challenged by the top management to set career goals, perform with excellence, obtain recognition for their accomplishments and sustain their career growth.

All employees must set goals which are measurable, expressed in a specific time frame, challenging and yet realistic. Employees are implored to set goals which are compatible with the organisation's own objectives.

It should also be explained that career goals do not necessarily have to move upwards only; career paths can also move horizontally or even downwards to start a new career.

All employees are expected to perform with excellence and do their utmost best to meet all the standards set when working towards their goals. Although many people are shy to talk of their own accomplishments because they do not want to be considered boastful, a distinction should be made between empty boasting and seeking recognition for genuine accomplishments.

Employees should be required to prepare reports of their achievements and activities and submit these reports to those people in the organisation who should know, for example, immediate superior, head of department, the human resource manager, etc. The employee's immediate

superior should be fully involved in guiding the employee. The organisation should provide developmental and educational opportunities so that employees are able to adapt to rapid changes in technology and business. When these opportunities are provided, it is then up to the individual to take advantage if he wants to develop his own career.

A comprehensive career development programme involves three main ingredients:

1. Assisting employees in assessing their own internal career needs;
2. Developing and publicising available career opportunities in the organisation; and
3. Aligning employee needs and abilities with career opportunities.

A person's career is a high personal and important element of his life. The basic stand of the organisation should be to provide all the guidance and help necessary but permit each person to make his own decision in this regard. The role of the human resource department is to assist employees in this decision-making process by providing as much information as possible through career counselling.

Many employees are often uncertain as to the type of work that would suit them best. By helping and providing some of the self-evaluation instruments already discussed above, the organisation can assist individuals in determining their primary interests and basic aptitudes to perform different types of work.

Some organisations provide formal assessment centre workshops or psychological personality profiling for employees using either internal experts or external consultants. With the aid of these experts, employees are helped to make decisions concerning proper career goals and specific development needs appropriate to those goals with the objective of helping employees to do their own planning.

Because all employees have definite career needs, there is a need for the organisation to chart specific career paths through the organisation for the information of employees. In jobs where there are only limited opportunities for significant progression, this should be identified and made known to possible applications so that only those employees who are heavily inclined towards security and who are not overly ambitious may find these jobs to be highly acceptable. Employees should be told what types of jobs are available now and in the immediate future, as well as in the medium and long-term. Information on the actual duties of these jobs, as well as the skills required and the type of training and development opportunities available for employees to acquire these skills should also be provided. Employees should be aware of how they can become eligible for training and development programmes and their selection criteria. It is also important for employees to know what jobs lead to other employment, that is, the career paths available.

In general terms, job analysis will provide the basic information required to chart the lines of promotion within an organisation. A careful analysis should be made of the duties of lower jobs to determine the suitability and adequacy of preparation for higher jobs. Unfortunately, in many organisations, the lines of advancement are restricted to within a single department and are generally obvious to anyone who studies the organisation chart. In fact, careful analysis of job duties will lead to the discovery of many alternative lines of advancement to several jobs in different areas.

When employees have accurately assessed their career needs and the organisational employment opportunities have been communicated to all employees, the remaining problem is one of alignment. All developmental training programmes can be incorporated into a planned career development programme as part of this alignment process.

Emphasis should also be given to individualised developmental programmes like special

assignments, planned job rotations and individual coaching by immediate superiors. The organisation's performance appraisal and management-by-objectives programmes should provide special focus on career progress and coaching needs as well as personal development objectives.

The final outcome of career development can be seen when the organisation makes specific transfer and promotion decisions for each employee. All the efforts of a career development programme will be meaningless if the employee does not progress along his individually-perceived career path.

ORGANIZATION'S CAREER DEVELOPMENT RESPONSIBILITIES

The boundary less career may redirect the primary responsibilities of career management to employees this does not mean the organizations have no responsibility. In the boundary less career, the organization's responsibility is to build employee self-reliance and to help employees maintain their marketability through continual learning. The organization needs to provide support for employees to continually add to their skills, abilities, and to their knowledge. The support includes:

1.Clearly communicating the organization's goals and future strategies:

When people know where the organization is headed, they are better equipped to develop a personal plan to share in that future.

2.Creating growth opportunities:

Employees should have the opportunity to get new interesting and professionally challenging work experience.

3.Offering financial assistance:

The Organization should offer tuition reimbursement to help employees keep up with current updates in management and technology.

4.Providing the time for employees to learn:

Organizations should be generous in providing paid time off from work for off-the-job training. In addition workloads should not be so demanding that they preclude employees from having the time to develop new skills, abilities and knowledge.

For example the Information Technology company in India Wipro has on site learning centers, where employees have unlimited access to personal development and educational books and periodicals, Videotapes and software. Unisys Corporation maintains a career website that helps employees assess their strengths and weaknesses, receive coaching and monitor their progress. An Australian leading Real estate company's all 4500 employees of "Lend Lease�? Receive

$1000 annually to spend on a variety of professional development activities including computer training and life planning coaching.

CAREER DEVELOPMENT SYSTEM

There are four steps in establishing a career development system. They are:

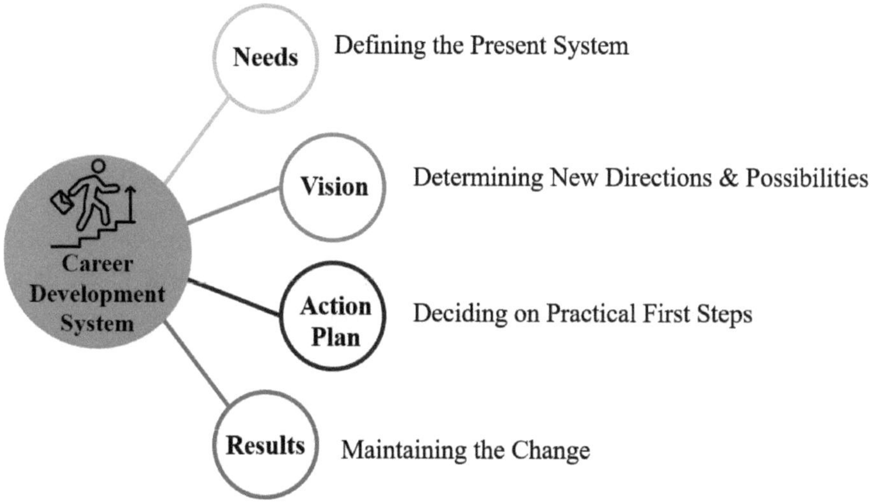

- Step 1. Needs: This step involves in the conducting a needs assessment as a training program.
- Step 2. Vision: The needs of the career system must be linked with the interventions. An ideal career development system known as the

vision links the needs with the interventions.

- Step 3. Action plan: An action plan should be formulated in order to achieve the vision. The support of the top management should be obtained in this process.
- Step 4. Results: Career development programs should be integrated with theorganization's on-going employee training and management development programs. The program should be evaluated from time to time in order to revise the program.

STEPS AND TASKS IN ESTABLISHING A CAREER DEVELOPMENT SYSTEM

Needs:

Defining the Present System and establish roles and responsibilities of employees, managers, and the organization. Identify needs; establish target groups.

Establish cultural parameters; determine organizational receptivity, support, and commitment to career development.

Assess existing HR programs or structures; consider possible links to a career development program.

Determine prior attempts at solving the problem or need.

Establish the mission or philosophy of the program. Design and implement needs assessment to confirm the data or collect more data. Establish indicators or criteria of success.

Vision:

Determine new direction and possibilities. Create a long-term philosophy and establish the vision or objectives of the program.

Design interventions for employees, managers, and the organization. Organize and make available career information needed to support the program.

Action plan:

Deciding on practical first Steps. Assess the plan and obtain support from top management. Create a pilot program.

Assess resources and competencies.

Establish an advisory group. Involve advisory group in data gathering, programs design, implementation, evaluation, and monitoring.

Results:

Maintaining the Change

Create long-term formalized approaches.

Publicize the program and evaluate and redesign the program and its components. Consider future trends and directions for the program.

Career development is essential to implement career plan. Career development consists of personal improvements undertaken by the individual employee, training, development and educational programs provided by the organization and various institutes. The most important aspect of career development is that every employee must accept his/her responsibility for development. Various career development actions prove useful if an employee is committed to career development.

Career Development Actions:

1. Job Performance: Employees must prove that his performance on the job is to the level of standards established, if he wants career progress.
2. Exposure: Employee's desire for career progress should expose their skills, knowledge, qualifications, achievements, performance etc. to those who take the decision about career progress.
3. Resignations: Employees may resign the present job in the organization, if they find that career opportunities elsewhere are better than those of the present organization.
4. Change the Job: Employees who put organizational loyalty above career loyalty may change the job in the same organization if they find that career opportunities in other jobs in the same organization are better than those in the present job.
5. Career Guidance: And counseling provides information, advice and encouragement to switch over to other career or organization, where career opportunities are better.

WHY DO ORGANIZATIONS NEED SUCCESSION PLANNING?

Both family run organizations as well as professionally run companies need succession planning although they may do so for different sets of reasons. For family run businesses, survival or change management is usually the predominant factor requiring a well thought out succession plan. For professionally run corporates, the single most important reason for having a sound succession plan in place is usually cost savings on account of (a) potential loss of business due to unfilled vacancies in key positions and (b) costs of external hiring and training. All the other reasons may be applicable to both types of organizations.

PRACTICES IN SUCCESSION PLANNING

The following best practices have proven valuable in guiding companies towards successful succession management:

Focus on Critical Positions

Organizations have traditionally focused succession planning on senior management positions. The present situation of talent shortage requires expanding succession planning to other critical positions that have the biggest impact on organizational performance. For example, in information technology it may be key developers, team leaders or project managers, in life sciences this may be key research and development staff; in utilities, field service workers critical to continuous service delivery; and in health care, nursing care professionals.

Integrate Employee Career Plans

An integrated approach focused on identifying and retaining talent must be supported by a solution that can seamlessly link an employee's career and development plan with the organisation's overall succession plans.

Encourage Proactive and Actionable Development Plans

Effective succession management relies on organizations to provide opportunities and proactive suggestions for development that increase the readiness of candidates for future positions. By linking learning and development with succession and career planning, organizations can positively impact the availability of talent to meet future requirements.

Evaluate Depth, Breadth and Cohesiveness of technology solutions

Investing in best-of-breed solutions that can expand to address the entire talent management life cycle — from developing to managing, optimizing, and rewarding — will enable organizations to maximize workforce productivity and ensure long-term business success. Web-based succession planning solutions provide timely, continuous access to processes and data, allowing employees to pro-actively "own" their career and development plans, straight from their own desktops.

By moving succession planning to the forefront of the corporate agenda and taking a proactive approach to leadership and employee development today, organizations are laying a

solid foundation for smooth leadership transitions in the future, thereby sidestepping the talent crisis.

Executed as part of an overall strategic talent management initiative, succession planning enables organizations to identify their current and future needs, and helps them align and develop talent accordingly. For succession to truly succeed, however, companies must focus on their employees' career development.

CHAPTER FIVE

FORECASTING

Once an assessment of the organization's current human resources situation has been made and the future direction of the organization in terms of revenue forecasts has been considered, a projection of future demand for human resources can be developed. Human resources demand is affected by an organization's environment. For example, the state of the economy can alter demand for a product or service and thus affect the need for certain types of employees. In addition to this, changing organizational requirements, can also influence the demand for human resources. Similarly, internal work force changes, such as retirements, resignations, terminations or deaths cause major shift in the need for human resources. Several basic techniques are used to forecast human resources demand. While judgmental forecasting is based mainly on the views of knowledgeable individuals, quantitative forecasting relies on numerical data and mathematical models. Finally, technological forecasting, aimed mainly at predicting long-term trends in technology can also help predict future demand.

Implications of Future Supply

Demand is only one side of the equation. Managers must also consider the other side—supply of sufficient human resources, to operate effectively. Managers consider both internal and external labor supplies. One prime source is a pool of current employees who can be transferred or promoted to help meet demands for human resources. Besides, internal labor supply, some reliance on the external labor supply is also necessary. Recent graduates from schools and colleges expand the supply of available human resources. Of particular importance in this category are women. Past high, levels of inflation and accelerating prices as well as changing attitude, aspirations and career expectations, have all acted as forces to increase the number of women entering the labor market.

Analyzing Sources of Supply of Human Resources

Manpower supply or Human resources supply is affected by various factors both internal and external. In this article we are discussing multiple situations leading to manpower requirements and supply.

After estimating future supply of human resources, sources of supply should be analyzed with a view to ensure the availability. Both internal and external factors affecting manpower supply should be analyzed.

Internal factors include: training facilities, salary levels, benefits, interpersonal relations, company programs, scope for self-advancement and growth, promotional opportunities, pride for creative and innovative ideas, providing challenge work etc.

The external factors are classified into local factors and national factors

Local Factors:

Population density in the area, local unemployment level, availability of employees on part-time, temporary and casual basis, current and future competition for the similar categories, outcome from local educational and training institutes, residential facilities available , local transport and communication facilities, traditional pattern of employment and availability of manpower with required qualification and skills, the pattern of migration and immigration, the attractiveness of the areas as a place to live, local housing, shopping, educational facilities, medical facilities, regulations of local government like reservation for local candidates, candidates belonging to scheduled, backward and minority communities etc.

National factors:

Trends in the growth of working population, training institutes and schemes in the country, outcome from technical, professional, vocational and general educational level, educational institutes in the country, migration and immigration patterns, social security measures (like unemployment benefits, lay-offs, retirement benefits etc.), cultural factors, customer, social norms etc., national demands for certain categories of manpower like technologists, scientists, management graduates, computer professionals etc., effect of changing educational patterns, impact of government, national educational policy, impact of government employment regulations such as reservation for candidates belonging to SC, ST and other categories.

Estimating the Net Human Resources Requirements:

Net human resource requirements in terms of number and components are to be determined in relation to the overall human resource requirements (demand forecast) for a future date and supply forecast for that date. The difference between overall human requirements and future supply of human resources is to be found out.

Action Plan for Redeployment, Redundancy/ Retrenchment

If future surplus is estimated, the organization has to plan for redeployment, redundancy etc. If surplus is estimated in some jobs/department, employees can be redeployed in other jobs/departments where the deficit of employees is estimated. Organization should also plan for training or reorientation before redeployment of employees. Redeployment takes place in the form of transfers. If the deficit is not estimated in any job/ department and surplus is estimated for the entire organization, the organization, in consultation with the trade unions, has to plan for redundancy or retrenchment.

Redundancy Plan:

Type and number of employees, time of and place of retrenchment, type of help to be extended to retrenched employees in the form of compensation, help in getting new job, priority in filling future vacancies.

Redeployment, Redundancy/Retrenchment Programs

The retrenchment and redundancy programs are as follows:

1.Outplacement:

Outplacement programs also intended to provide career guidance for displaced employees. This programs covers retraining the prospective displaced employees who can be redeployed elsewhere in the organization, helping in resume writing, interview techniques, job searching.

2.Layoffs:

Layoffs can be temporary or permanent. Temporary layoffs are due to the slackness in business, machinery breakage, power failure etc. Workers are called back as soon as work resumes to the normal position. Permanent layoff is due to liquidation of the company. Proper human resource planning leaving the workforce at proper level can help to reduce this effect.

3.Leave of Absence without Pay:

This technique helps the company to cut the labor cost and the employee to pursue his self- interests. This technique also helps the company to plan for eliminating the unnecessary job in a phased manner. This concept serves or a productive method to help employees prepare for future changes.

4.Work Sharing:

Some organizations offer employees the opportunity to share jobs or two employees working one-half time each. This technique solves the problem of retrenchment in the short run. This is in vogue in advanced countries but not acceptable to workers' unions in most Asian counties.

5.Reduced Working Hours:

Under this technique, each worker, works less hours, and receives less pay, so that two jobs are saved. Again this is not prevalent in Asian countries and other developing countries.

6.Voluntary/ Early Retirement:

Another issue is early retirement. Government of India introduced Voluntary Retirement Scheme under the caption 'Golden Handshake' in order to solve the problem of over staffing in Public sector. This technique solves the problem of excessive supply of future inventory over the demand for the human resources. In short it is popularly called as VRS.

7.Attrition:

Attrition is the process whereby the existing employees leave their jobs for various reasons. Those jobs will be kept vacant or unfilled. Attrition or hiring freezes or ban on employment can be implemented organization-wide or department-wise or job-wise if the HR manager forecasts a surplus manpower in the organization. But if the attrition rate is continuous and high then it is high time the concerned authorities in the organization have introspection and take remedial actions. High Attrition is a sign of bad reputation for the organization as a working place.

8.Reconciling Demand and Supply

After estimating the demand and supply of human resources managers must often take steps to balance the two. If estimates show that the internal supply of labor is too large, then managers need to make plans to reduce the numbers of employees through measures such as resignations and retirements, or voluntary retirement schemes. On the other hand, if additional employees are necessary, then plans must be made for promoting and transferring current organization members and for hiring new workers. Thus, the objective of human resources planning is to bring together forecast of future demand and supply. The result of this effort will be to pinpoint shortages both in number and in quality and to highlight areas where over staffing may exist

Process of Human Resources Planning

Process of Human Resources Planning consists of the following steps:

1. Analyzing organizational plans.
2. Demand Forecasting: forecasting the overall human resources requirements in accordance with the organizational plans.
3. Supply Forecasting : Obtaining the data and information about the present inventory of human resources and forecast the future changes in the human resources inventory.
4. Estimating the net human resources requirements.
5. In case of future surplus, plan for redeployment, retrenchment and lay-off.
6. In case of future deficit, forecast the future supply of human resources from all sources with reference to plans of other companies.
7. Plan for recruitment, development and internal mobility if future supply is more than or equal to net human resources requirements.
8. Plan to modify or adjust the organizational plan if future supply will be inadequate with reference to future net requirements.

The eight steps of human resources planning are depicted in the figure given below in the order mentioned above .But the same order need not be followed in the actual planning process as the steps are interdependent and sometimes, the first step and the last step may be processed simultaneously .And the planner sometimes may not explicitly process some steps .However, it is helped to the planner to plan for HR effectively without any complications if he/she has an idea about all steps of HRP. These are discussed in detail given below.

Analyzing the Organizational Plans

The process of human resources planning should start with analyzing the organizational plan into production plan, technological plan, plans for expansion, diversification etc. Marketing plan, sales plan financial plan .Each plan can be further analyzed into sub units. Detailed programs should be formulated on the basis of unit-wise plans. Practicability of each programs should be ensured .Analysis of organizational plans and programs helps in forecasting the demand for human resources as it provides the quantum of future work activity.

Forecasting the Overall Human Resources Requirements

The jobs should be redesigned and reanalyzed keeping in view the organizational and unit-wise plans and programs, future work quantum, future activity or task analysis. Future skills values, knowledge and capabilities of present employees and prospective employees. Job analysis and forecasts about the future components of HR facilitate demand forecasting .One of the important aspects of demand forecasting is the forecasting of the quality of human resources (skill knowledge values, capabilities etc. In addition to quantity of human resources.

Important forecasting methods are:

1.Managerial Judgement

Small organizations resort to the management –judgement approach. This method the managers or supervisors who are well acquainted with the workload efficiency and ability of employees think about their future workload, future capabilities of employees and decide on the number and type of HR to be required. The management at the top compares the proposals with the organizational plans makes necessary arrangements and finalizes the plans. Alternatively this exercise can also be done by the top management which in turn sends the information at the top prepares the organizational plans, departmental plans and human resources plans. But the best approach is participative approach, where both the management at the top and supervisors at the bottom meet and decide on the human resources needs based on the experience of the supervisors and the plans formulated by the top officials.

2.Trend Analysis

Trend Analysis refers to a method which involves studying variations in your company's employment levels over a period of the last few years in order to arrive at the future needs. In this, you can compute the number of employees in your company at the end of each year in the last 5 years or the number of employees in each department at the end of each of the years. In this way, you would be able to work out a trend which may continue in the future. This analysis can provide an initial estimate. However, you need to remember that the employee level in the company also depends on other factors like sales volume, productivity, future company expansion plans, etc.

3.Ratio Analysis

Ratio Analysis means making forecasts based on the ratio between

1. Factors like sales volume
2. No. of employees required (example sales force)

For example, if a sales person generates Rs. 5,00,000 in sales. Your company wants to target a sales turnover of Rs. 1 crore, then a simple ratio calculation would show that you would require 20 sales persons in the next year (with an average generation of Rs. 5,00,000 per annum)

Like trend analysis, ratio analysis assumes that productivity of each sales person remains the same, i.e., their performance would not exceed Rs. 5,00,000. If the productivity had to increase or decrease, then the ratio would also accordingly change.

4. Scatter Plot Method

This method shows the relationship between two different variables – such as level of turnover of the company and the employment level within the company. If the two variables are related, then it would be possible to forecast the manpower requirement on the basis of the targeted growth in revenue of the company in the future.

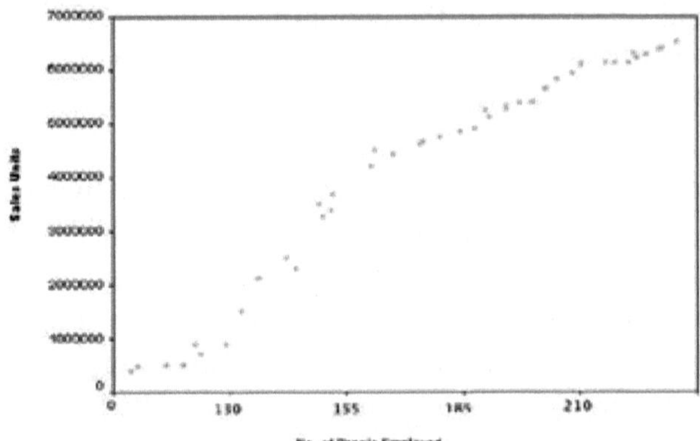
7000000
6000000
5000000
4000000
3000000
2000000
1000000
0
Sales Units
0
130
155
185
210
No. of People Employed

CHAPTER SIX

BUDGETING

Most firms do not have a line item in the annual budget devoted exclusively to recruitment. Those dollars are usually scrounged from the general human resources kitty. This isn't surprising since, up until a few years ago, recruitment was a straightforward, administrative process: You went to your resume files (or ran an ad to beef them up), picked out the handful with qualifications that matched your hiring need, interviewed some people, and, presto—you had a new staff person. More recently, smart firms have realized that their exciting marketing and promotional efforts (and dollars) actually help them attract good people.

Recruitment is no longer an administrative aspect of your human resources function. It requires fully dedicated labor and dollars in order for growing firms to meet their goals. And, like most expenditures, recruitment costs are easier for management to swallow when they're anticipated. Make educated guesses as to how much money you'll need to get the next fiscal year's recruitment efforts off the ground. And be liberal.

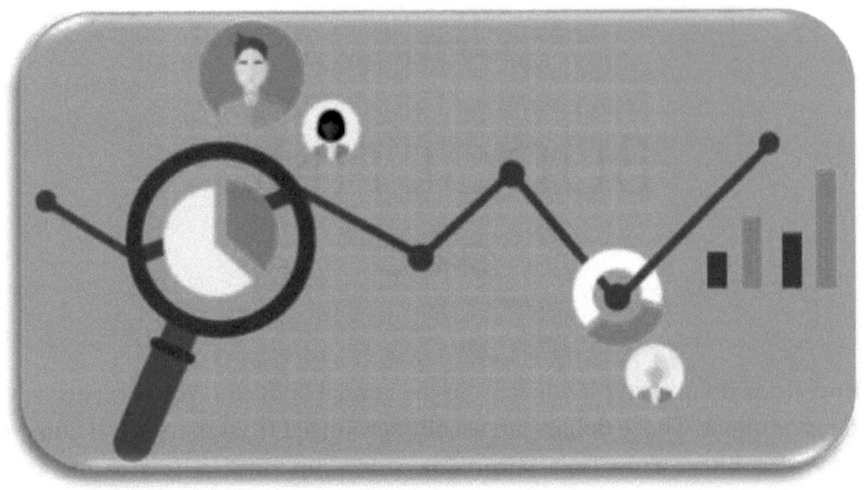

RECRUITMENT BUDGETING CONSIDERATIONS AND BEST PRACTICES:

1. Examine the advertising resources and carefully choose days to place advertisements. It is not advisable to advertise positions during the week as most job seekers examine weekend publications for job announcements. It is also advisable to ask the newspaper resources if they post their advertisements on the web or with affiliate job search engines.
2. Consider the costs of lodging, meals and travel as the search and hire process is executed.
3. Evaluate the number of qualified candidates invited to interview. Carefully screening and selecting candidates for interviews will assist in managing budgeting resources wisely. Phone screening is highly recommended.
4. Plan interviews in a manner that capitalizes on getting the most accomplished in the least amount of days. Interviews spanning several days results in increased travel, food, and lodging dollars.
5. Assess the costs associated with additional meetings outside the formal interview. Plan meetings that are informal in nature and do not require

"sit down" meals or excessive travel to various locations.

6. Focus on candidates meeting with key personnel with whom they will work. Once a candidate begins working, there will be time for department-wide introductions and meetings. Focusing on key personnel will eliminate additional costs associated with meals, travel and lodging.

CHAPTER SEVEN

COMPETENCE MAPPING

Competency mapping is important and is an essential exercise. Every well managed firm should: have well defined roles and list of competencies required to perform each role effectively.

The competency framework serves as the bedrock for all HR applications. As a result of competency mapping, all the HR processes like talent induction, management development, appraisals and training yield much better results.

WHAT IS A COMPETENCY?

Competency as a cluster of related knowledge, attitudes, skills and other personal characteristics that:

- Affects a major part of one's job
- Correlates with performance on the job
- Can be measured against well-accepted standards
- Can be improved via training and development

DEFINITION

"Competency is an underlying characteristic of an individual that is causally related to criterion referenced effective and/or superior performance in a job or a situation." -"McClelland"

CATEGORIES OF COMPETENCIES IN ORGANIZATIONS

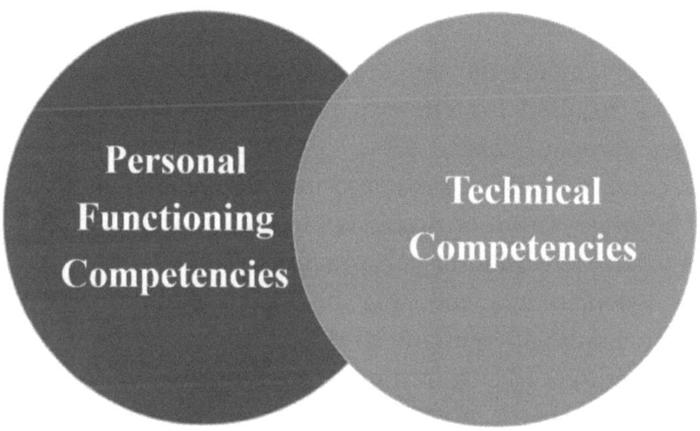

1. Personal Functioning Competencies: These competencies include broad success factors not tied to a specific work function or industry (often focusing on leadership or emotional intelligence behaviors).
2. Functional/Technical Competencies: These competencies include specific success factors within a given work function or industry.

WHAT IS COMPETENCY PROFILING?

Competency profiling is the process of identifying the knowledge, skills, abilities, attitudes, and judgment required for effective performance in a particular occupation or profession.

Competency profiling is business/company specific.

WHAT IS COMPETENCY MAPPING?

Competency mapping is the process of identification of the competencies required to perform successfully a given job or role or a set of tasks at a given point of time. It consists of breaking a given role or job into its constituent tasks or activities and identifying the competencies (technical, managerial, behavioral, conceptual knowledge, an attitudes, skills, etc.) needed to perform the same successfully.

WHAT IS A COMPETENCY MODEL?

A competency model is an organizing framework that lists the competencies required for effective performance in a specific job, job family (e.g., group of related jobs), organization, function, or process. Individual competencies are organized into competency models to enable people in an organization or profession to understand, discuss, and apply the competencies to workforce performance.

The competencies in a model may be organized in a variety of formats. No one approach is inherently best; organizational needs will determine the optimal framework. A common approach is to identify several competencies that are essential for all employees and then identify several additional categories of competencies that apply only to specific subgroups. Some competency models are organized according to the type of competency, such as leadership, personal effectiveness, or technical capacity. Other models may employ a framework based on job level, with a basic set of competencies for a given job family and additional competencies added cumulatively for each higher job level within the job family.

AREA OF IMPLEMENTATION

1. **Recruitment and Selection**

Choosing the right people to join and progress in an organization.

Competencies can be used to construct a template for using in recruitment and selection. Information on the level of a competency required for effective performance would be used to determine the competency levels that new hires should possess.

Depending upon the accepted definition, competency data may take the form of behaviors, skills, abilities and other characteristics that have been associated with effective

1.Training and Development

Identifying gaps and helping employees develop in the right direction.

Knowing the competency profile for a position allows individuals to compare their own competencies to those required by the position or the career path. Training or development plans could focus on those competencies needing improvement. Additionally education and development curricula would be linked to improving competency levels to the needed levels needed for effective performance.

2.Career and Succession Planning

Assessing employees' readiness or potential to take on new challenges

Determining a person job fit can be based on matching the competency profile of an individual to the set of competencies required for excellence within a profession. Individuals would know the competencies required for a particular position and therefore would have an opportunity to decide if they have the potential to pursue that position.

3.Rewards and Recognition

Competency based pay is compensation for individual characteristics for skills and competencies over and above the pay a job or organizational role itself commands. Individual characteristics that merit higher pay may come in the form of competencies (experience, initiative, loyalty and memory portability).

One old fashioned way of improving employee performance is by recognizing and rewarding effort. Competency pay is the best way to do so. Rewarding employees for their ability to make the best use of their skills and competencies in accordance with the organization's needs was the logic behind this once popular HR tool.

4.Performance Management System

Competencies are critical behaviors demonstrated on the job and, as such, are often included as part of performance management. Performance management is about achieving results in a manner that is consistent with organizational expectations and desired behaviors. Competencies provide expectations for "how" the job is performed, not just "what" gets done. Assessing competencies as a part of performance management is an important means of assisting employees in understanding performance expectations and enhancing competencies on-the-job. Most departments have their own performance management systems. Competencies may play an important role in these systems.

BENEFITS AND CRITICISM OF COMPETENCY PROFILING

Benefits:

- Employees have a set of objectives to work towards and are clear about how they are expected to perform their jobs.
- The appraisal and recruitment systems are fairer and more open.
- There is a link between organizational and personal objectives.
- Processes are measurable and standardized across organizational and geographical boundaries.
- It gives a clear insight in the necessary qualifications for a job and therefore;
- Provides a common language for discussing job requirements and/or individuals' capabilities;
- Increases identifying the best resources to fill a given role
- Provides a tool to help an employee, manager or organization assess its competencies and identify its future needs;\
- Ensures the link between business strategy and Human Resource functions;
- Allows strategic-level tracking of the collective strengths and areas of expertise within an organization.

Criticism:

- It can be over-elaborate and bureaucratic.
- It is difficult to strike the right balance between reviewing the competencies often enough for them to remain relevant but not so often as to become confusing.
- If too much emphasis is placed on 'inputs' at the expense of 'outputs', there is a risk that it will favor employees who are good in theory but not in practice and will fail to achieve the results that make a business successful.

- They can become out of date very quickly due to the fast pace of change in organizations and it can therefore be expensive and time consuming to keep them up-to-date. .

- Some behavioral competencies are basically personality traits which an individual may be unable (or unwilling) to change and it is not reasonable to judge someone on these rather than what he or she actually achieves.

METHODOLOGY ADOPTED

Step 1: Identify Departments for Competency Profiling

Here we have to decide and select the departments within the organization which we would like to include into our study. It is to be noted that departments should be chosen based on their criticality and importance to the organization.

For example, in the Company XYZ, there are 10 departments

For this project all departments have been considered except the four support functions namely being the information management department, human resource department, engineering department and Purchase Department functions.

Step 2: Identifying Hierarchy within the Organization and Selection of Levels

Study the organization hierarchy across each of the selected departments. For the purpose of the study at Company XYZ we have selected Senior Management (Assistant General Manager), Middle Management (Group leader/Research Associate/Manager) and Junior Management (Scientist II Executive).

Step 3: Obtain the Job Descriptions.

For all three levels at every department we obtained each role's job description and in cases where they were not available we conducted a detailed interview to derive a job description.

Step 4 Preparation of Semi-Structured Interview

As one of the tools for collecting information we prepared a list of questions that would make up a semi structured interview. These questions would be put forth employee's at all three management levels.

Step 5: Scheduling of Interviews

Obtain a list of employees from respective department heads and accordingly schedule interviews. A minimum of 5 candidates are to be interviewed at each level in each department.

Step 6: Conducting of Interviews

We would have to arrange for the semi structured interviews to be carried out at a convenient time and comfortable location as per the candidate's convenience.

Step 7 ;Recording of Interview Details

The candidate's answers and opinions have to be recorded in as much detail as possible for further reference during the project.

Step 8: Preparation of a List of Skills

As per the interview and the details that were generated from the candidate, we will generate a list of skills observed for the job. Thereon from which a list of identified competencies should be drawn for each interviewed candidate.

Step 9: Repeat for Next Levels and Functions.

The interviews and appropriate recording of answers should be done at all remaining levels and other departments within the Company XYZ

Step 10: Make the list of the Competencies required for the Department for each level and each function giving Behavioral Indicators.

For each position at each department a list of competencies observed from both the job description and the semi structured interview (list of skills) should be drawn up.

Each competency should be given a name and an appropriate definition that clearly indicates its meaning and essence.

Step 11: Indicate Proficiency Levels

Take one competency at a time and indicate different proficiency levels. For the project four levels of proficiency had to be defined for every competency. Each proficiency level was defined in term of behavioral indicators.

Step 12: Validate identified Competencies and Proficiency levels with Head of Departments.

Confirm competency definitions with respective Head Of Departments and obtain from the required proficiency levels of each competency that is ideal for each role. Also locate any missing competencies.

Step 13: Preparation of competency matrix

Prepare a matrix defining competencies required and corresponding proficiency levels for each level across all departments.

Step 14: Mapping of Competencies

Mapping of competencies of selected employees against the competency matrix as per their employee level and department. Here an employee's actual proficiency level of a particular competency would be mapped against the target proficiency level.

9 798885 913775

Printed by Libri Plureos GmbH in Hamburg,
Germany